UNLOCK

Second Edition

1

Reading, Writing & Critical Thinking

STUDENT'S BOOK

Sabina Ostrowska and Kate Adams
with Chris Sowton, Jessica Williams
and Christina Cavage

CAMBRIDGE
UNIVERSITY PRESS

CAMBRIDGE
UNIVERSITY PRESS

University Printing House, Cambridge CB2 8BS, United Kingdom

One Liberty Plaza, 20th Floor, New York, NY 10006, USA

477 Williamstown Road, Port Melbourne, VIC 3207, Australia

314–321, 3rd Floor, Plot 3, Splendor Forum, Jasola District Centre, New Delhi – 110025, India

79 Anson Road, #06–04/06, Singapore 079906

Cambridge University Press is part of the University of Cambridge.

It furthers the University's mission by disseminating knowledge in the pursuit of education, learning and research at the highest international levels of excellence.

www.cambridge.org
Information on this title: www.cambridge.org/9781108681612

© Cambridge University Press 2019

First published 2014
Second Edition 2019

20 19 18 17 16 15 14 13 12 11 10 9 8 7 6 5 4 3 2 1

Printed in Dubai by Oriental Press

A catalogue record for this publication is available from the British Library

ISBN 978-1-108-68161-2 Reading, Writing and Critical Thinking Student's Book, Mobile App & Online Workbook 1 with Downloadable Video

CONTENTS

UNIT	VIDEO	READING	VOCABULARY	
1 PEOPLE Reading 1: A profile of a famous person (Communications) Reading 2: A very tall man! (Anthropology)	Fishermen	**_Key reading skill:_** Previewing a text **_Additional skills:_** Understanding key vocabulary Skimming Scanning to find information Reading for detail Understanding key vocabulary Synthesizing	Family vocabulary	
2 SEASONS Reading 1: An article about the coldest city in the world (Geography) Reading 2: Cuban climate and weather (Meteorology)	The taiga forest	**_Key reading skill:_** Scanning to find information **_Additional skills:_** Using your knowledge Understanding key vocabulary Reading for detail Previewing Synthesizing	Vocabulary for climate, weather and seasons	
3 LIFESTYLE Reading 1: Meet the Kombai (Anthropology) Reading 2: Student timetable (Sociology / Education)	Toronto tourism	**_Key reading skill:_** Annotating a text **_Additional skills:_** Using your knowledge Understanding key vocabulary Scanning to find information Reading for main ideas Previewing Synthesizing	Collocations for free-time activities Vocabulary for study	
4 PLACES Reading 1: A world history of maps (History) Reading 2: The Maldives (Geography)	The _cenotes_ of Mexico	**_Key reading skill:_** Reading for main ideas **_Additional skills:_** Understanding key vocabulary Previewing Annotating Scanning to find information Reading for detail Using your knowledge Synthesizing	Vocabulary for places	

GRAMMAR	CRITICAL THINKING	WRITING
Nouns and verbs *Grammar for writing:* Subject pronouns The verb *be* Possessive adjectives	Collecting information	*Academic writing skill:* Writing simple sentences: • subject + verb • capital letters • full stops *Writing task type:* Write descriptive sentences *Writing task:* Write a profile of your family.
Nouns and adjectives Noun phrases *Grammar for writing:* Prepositional phrases	Categorizing information	*Academic writing skills:* Word order: subject–verb–adjective Punctuation: • capital letters • commas *Writing task type:* Write descriptive sentences *Writing task:* Write about the weather in your city or town.
Time expressions *Grammar for writing:* Parts of a sentence The present simple	Choosing relevant information	*Academic writing skill:* Main ideas and details *Writing task type:* Write descriptive sentences *Writing task:* Write about the life of a student in your class.
Noun phrases with *of* *Grammar for writing:* *There is / There are* Articles	Classifying topics and key words	*Academic writing skills:* Spelling and punctuation: capital letters Paragraph structure: topic sentences *Writing task type:* Write a descriptive paragraph *Writing task:* Write facts about your country.

UNIT	VIDEO	READING	VOCABULARY	
5 JOBS Reading 1: Find_my_job.com (Business and management) Reading 2: Job emails (Business and management)	Utah's Bingham mine	_Key reading skill:_ Reading for detail _Additional skills:_ Using your knowledge Previewing Understanding key vocabulary Scanning to find information Reading for main ideas Synthesizing	Vocabulary for jobs	
6 HOMES AND BUILDINGS Reading 1: Architect's world: expert interview (Architecture) Reading 2: Skyscrapers (Architecture)	Living in Singapore	_Key reading skill:_ Predicting content using visuals _Additional skills:_ Using your knowledge Understanding key vocabulary Scanning to find information Reading for main ideas Reading for detail Synthesizing	Vocabulary for buildings	
7 FOOD AND CULTURE Reading 1: Tea: A world history (History) Reading 2: Ten of the best by cuisine (Hospitality management)	Goat's cheese	_Key reading skills:_ Skimming Taking notes _Additional skills:_ Using your knowledge Understanding key vocabulary Reading for main ideas Reading for detail Scanning to find information Previewing Synthesizing	Vocabulary for food and drink	
8 TRANSPORT Reading 1: Transport survey (Transport and logistics) Reading 2: Transport in Bangkok: Report (Urban planning)	Modern metros	_Key reading skill:_ Working out meaning from context _Additional skills:_ Previewing Understanding key vocabulary Skimming Scanning to find information Reading for detail Using your knowledge Reading for main ideas Synthesizing	Transport collocations	

GRAMMAR	CRITICAL THINKING	WRITING
Adjective phrases *Grammar for writing:* *Must* and *have to* The pronoun *you*	Analyzing and evaluating opinions	*Academic writing skills:* Joining sentences with *and*: • simple sentences • compound sentences Writing an email *Writing task type:* Write an email *Writing task:* Write an email about a job.
Pronouns Adjectives *Grammar for writing:* Comparing quantities Comparative adjectives	Analyzing data	*Academic writing skills:* Compound sentences with *but* Spelling: double consonants Supporting sentences *Writing task type:* Write a comparative paragraph *Writing task:* Write a comparison of two buildings.

Countable and
  uncountable nouns
Can and *cannot*
Grammar for writing:
Subject–verb agreement
Determiners: *a*, *an* and
  some
	Generating ideas	*Academic writing skills:*
		Error correction
		Concluding sentences
		Writing task type:
		Write a descriptive paragraph
		Writing task:
		Write about popular food in your country.

Superlative adjectives
Quantifiers
Grammar for writing:
Subject–verb–object
Linking sentences with
  pronouns
	Collecting and analyzing data	*Academic writing skill:*
		Giving reasons with *because* and results with *so*
		Writing task type:
		Write an explanatory paragraph
		Writing task:
		Write a paragraph explaining the results of a
		  survey about transport.

Unlock your academic potential

Unlock Second Edition is a six-level, academic-light English course created to build the skills and language students need for their studies (CEFR Pre-A1 to C1). It develops students' ability to think critically in an academic context right from the start of their language learning. Every level has 100% new inspiring video on a range of academic topics.

Confidence in teaching.
Joy in learning.

Better Learning WITH UNL⌀CK SECOND EDITION

Better Learning is our simple approach where insights we've gained from research have helped shape content that drives results. We've listened to teachers all around the world and made changes so that *Unlock* Second Edition better supports students along the way to academic success.

CRITICAL THINKING

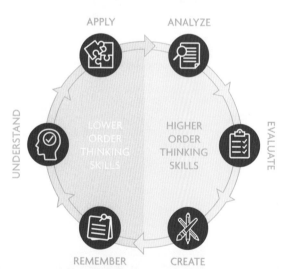

APPLY — ANALYZE — UNDERSTAND — EVALUATE — LOWER ORDER THINKING SKILLS — HIGHER ORDER THINKING SKILLS — REMEMBER — CREATE

Critical thinking in *Unlock* Second Edition …

- is **informed** by a range of academic research from Bloom in the 1950s, to Krathwohl and Anderson in the 2000s, to more recent considerations relating to 21st Century Skills
- has a **refined** syllabus with a better mix of higher- and lower-order critical thinking skills
- is **measurable**, with objectives and self-evaluation so students can track their critical thinking progress
- is **transparent** so teachers and students know when and why they're developing critical thinking skills
- is **supported** with professional development material for teachers so teachers can teach with confidence

… so that students have the best possible chance of academic success.

INSIGHT

Most classroom time is currently spent on developing lower-order critical thinking skills. Students need to be able to use higher-order critical thinking skills too.

CONTENT

Unlock Second Edition includes the right mix of lower- and higher-order thinking skills development in every unit, with clear learning objectives.

RESULTS

Students are better prepared for their academic studies and have the confidence to apply the critical thinking skills they have developed.

CLASSROOM APP

The *Unlock* Second Edition Classroom App ...

- offers extra, **motivating** practice in speaking, critical thinking and language
- provides a **convenient** bank of language and skills reference informed by our exclusive Corpus research ⊙
- is easily **accessible** and **navigable** from students' mobile phones
- is fully **integrated** into every unit
- provides Unlock-**specific** activities to extend the lesson whenever you see this symbol 📱

... so that students can easily get the right, extra practice they need, when they need it.

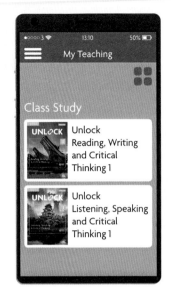

INSIGHT

The learning material on a Classroom app is most effective when it's an integral, well-timed part of a lesson.

CONTENT

Every unit of *Unlock* Second Edition is enhanced with bespoke Classroom app material to extend the skills and language students are learning in the book. The symbol 📱 shows when to use the app.

RESULTS

Students are motivated by having relevant extension material on their mobile phones to maximize their language learning. Teachers are reassured that the Classroom App adds real language-learning value to their lessons.

RESEARCH

We have gained deeper insights to inform *Unlock* Second Edition by ...

- carrying out **extensive market research** with teachers and students to fully understand their needs throughout the course's development
- consulting **academic research** into critical thinking
- refining our vocabulary syllabus using our **exclusive Corpus research** ⊙

... so that you can be assured of the quality of *Unlock* Second Edition.

INSIGHT

- Consultation with global Advisory Panel
- Comprehensive reviews of material
- Face-to-face interviews and Skype™ calls
- Classroom observations

CONTENT

- Improved critical thinking
- 100% new video and video lessons
- Clearer contexts for language presentation and practice
- Text-by-text glossaries
- More supportive writing sections
- Online Workbooks with more robust content
- Comprehensive teacher support

RESULTS

"Thank you for all the effort you've put into developing Unlock Second Edition. As far as I can see, I think the new edition is more academic and more appealing to young adults."

Burçin Gönülsen,
Işık Üniversity, Turkey

Unlock your knowledge

Encourages discussion around the themes of the unit with inspiration from interesting questions and striking images.

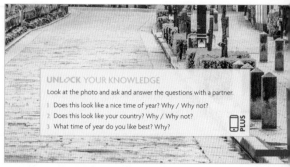

Watch and listen

Features an engaging and motivating video which generates interest in the topic and develops listening skills.

READING

Reading 1

The first text offers students the opportunity to develop the reading skills required to process academic texts, and presents and practises the vocabulary needed to comprehend the text itself.

Reading 2

Presents a second text which provides a different angle on the topic and serves as a model text for the writing task.

Language development

Consolidates and expands on the language presented in preparation for the writing task.

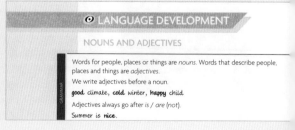

WRITING

Critical thinking

Develops the lower- and higher-order thinking skills required for the writing task.

Grammar for writing

Presents and practises grammatical structures and features needed for the writing task.

Academic writing skills

Practises all the writing skills needed for the writing task.

Writing task

Uses the skills and language learned throughout the unit to support students in drafting, producing and editing a piece of academic writing. This is the unit's main learning objective.

Objectives review

Allows students to evaluate how well they have mastered the skills covered in the unit.

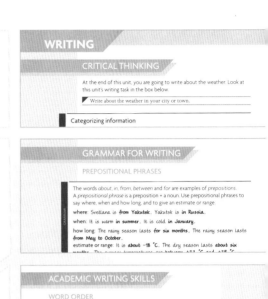

Wordlist

Lists the key vocabulary from the unit. The most frequent words used at this level in an academic context are highlighted. ⊙

Unlock offers 56 hours per Student's Book, which is extendable to 90 hours with the Classroom App, Online Workbook and other additional activities in the Teacher's Manual and Development Pack.

Unlock is a paired-skills course with two separate Student's Books per level. For levels 1–5 (CEFR A1 – C1), these are **Reading, Writing and Critical Thinking** and **Listening, Speaking and Critical Thinking**. They share the same unit topics so you have access to a wide range of material at each level. Each Student's Book provides access to the Classroom App and Online Workbook.

Unlock Basic has been developed for pre-A1 learners. **Unlock Basic Skills** integrates reading, writing, listening, speaking and critical thinking in one book to provide students with an effective and manageable learning experience. **Unlock Basic Literacy** develops and builds confidence in literacy. The *Basic* books also share the same unit topics and so can be used together or separately, and **Unlock Basic Literacy** can be used for self-study.

Student components

Resource	Description	Access

Student's Books	• Levels 1–5 come with Classroom App, Online Workbook, and downloadable audio and video
	    – Levels 1–4 (8 units)
	    – Level 5 (10 units)
	 • *Unlock Basic Skills* comes with downloadable audio and video (11 units)
	 • *Unlock Basic Literacy* comes with downloadable audio (11 units)
		• The Classroom App and Online Workbook are on the **CLMS** and are accessed via the unique code inside the front cover of the Student's Book
		 • The audio and video are downloadable from the Resources tab on the **CLMS**

Online Workbook	• Levels 1–5 only • Extension activities to further practise the language and skills learned • All-new vocabulary activities in the Online Workbooks practise the target vocabulary in new contexts	• The Online Workbook is on the **CLMS** and is accessed via the unique code inside the front cover of the Student's Book
Classroom App	• Levels 1–5 only • Extra practice in speaking, critical thinking and language	• The app is downloadable from the **Apple App Store** or **Google Play** • Students use the same login details as for the **CLMS**, and then they are logged in for a year
Video	• Levels 1–5 and *Unlock Basic Skills* only • All the video from the course	• The video is downloadable from the Resources tab on the **CLMS**
Audio	• All the audio from the course	• The audio is downloadable from the Resources tab on the **CLMS** and from **cambridge.org/unlock**

Teacher components

Resource	Description	Access
Teacher's Manual and Development Pack	• One manual covers Levels 1–5 • It contains flexible lesson plans, lesson objectives, additional activities and common learner errors as well as professional development for teachers, *Developing critical thinking skills in your students* • It comes with downloadable audio and video, vocabulary worksheets and peer-to-peer teacher training worksheets	• The audio, video and worksheets are downloadable from the Resources tab on the **CLMS** and from **eSource** via the code inside the front cover of the manual
Presentation Plus	• Software for interactive whiteboards so you can present the pages of the Student's Books and easily play audio and video, and check answers	• Please contact your sales rep for codes to download Presentation Plus from **eSource**

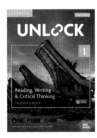

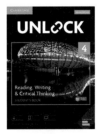

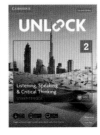

LEARNING OBJECTIVES	IN THIS UNIT YOU WILL ...
Watch and listen	watch and understand a video about people who catch fish in different countries.
Reading skill	preview a text.
Critical thinking	collect information.
Grammar	use nouns and verbs; use subject pronouns; use the verb *be*; use possessive adjectives.
Academic writing skill	write simple sentences.
Writing task	write a profile.

UNL⌀CK YOUR KNOWLEDGE

Ask and answer the questions with a partner.

1 What is your name?
2 Where do you live?
3 Do you have a job? What do you do?
4 Do you study? What do you study?

PLUS

WATCH AND LISTEN

PREPARING TO WATCH

ACTIVATING YOUR
KNOWLEDGE

1 Work with a partner and answer the questions.

1 What do you like to eat? How often do you eat fish?
2 Think about people who live by the sea. What jobs do they have? What do they do in their free time?
3 Where can you buy or eat fish?

PREDICTING
CONTENT USING
VISUALS

2 Match the sentences (1–4) with the pictures from the video.

1 The fishing boat is on the sea.
2 The fisherman is smiling.
3 They are fishing from a bridge.
4 They are eating fish in a restaurant.

GLOSSARY

---

coast (n) the land close to the sea

net (n) a thin kind of cloth for fishing

population (n) all the people who live in a country

relax (v) to become happy and comfortable

fishing rod (n) a long piece of wood that is used for fishing

WHILE WATCHING

UNDERSTANDING
MAIN IDEAS

3 ▶ Watch the video. Tick (✔) the information that you hear.

☐ 1 Fish is a healthy food.
☐ 2 Fishing is a difficult job.
☐ 3 Fishing is a popular sport all over the world.
☐ 4 For some people, fishing is a job.
☐ 5 Fish and chips is popular in the UK.
☐ 6 Fishing is a good way to relax with friends.

4 ▶ Watch again. Circle the words you hear.

1 We eat 100,000 *kilograms* / *tonnes* of fish every year.
2 Most fishing boats are *small* / *slow*.
3 The fishermen in India use fishing *rods* / *nets* to catch their fish.
4 There are more than *10,000* / *100,000* fish and chip shops in the UK.

5 Tick (✔) the true statements from the video.

☐ 1 Fishermen are catching more fish today than in the past.
☐ 2 Most fishing boats have only one fisherman on them.
☐ 3 Most of the people on the bridge are fishing for fun, not as their job.
☐ 4 You can find a fish and chip shop in many towns in the UK.
☐ 5 There are different ways to catch fish.
☐ 6 Most fishing boats are big.

DISCUSSION

6 Work with a partner and answer the questions.

1 Do you think fishing is an easy or hard job? Explain your answer.
2 Would you like to live in a village or town near the sea?
  Why / Why not?
3 Do you think fishing is a good job for a man or a woman?
  Why / Why not?

READING

PREPARING TO READ

SKILLS

Previewing a text

Previewing means looking at a text before you read it. When you preview a text, look at the text and think about these questions:

1 Are there photos?
2 What is in the photos?
3 What is the title of the text?
4 Where is the text from? (a book? a magazine? a website?)

PREVIEWING

1 Look at the photo and the text on page 19. Ask and answer the questions with a partner.

1 What do you think the text is about?
2 What is a profile? Where can you find profiles?
3 Look at the photo. Who do you think Moeen Ali is?

UNDERSTANDING
KEY VOCABULARY

2 You are going to read a profile of a famous cricket player. Read the words and examples in the table. Then write the bold words from the table in the sentences (1–6) below.

words	examples
languages	Spanish, Urdu, Russian
city	New York, Dubai, Tokyo, Istanbul
date of birth	4 May 1998
country	Saudi Arabia, the United Kingdom, China, Thailand
job	teacher, doctor
hobbies	reading, watching football, running

1 London is a very big _____ in England. Many people live there.
2 I speak three _____ : Turkish, Arabic and English.
3 Morocco is a _____ in North Africa. It is close to Algeria and Spain.
4 My _____ is 7 July 1997.
5 I have a great _____ . I am a teacher.
6 I have many _____ . I like running, reading and watching cricket.

My Profile

Moeen Ali

My personal information

First name: Moeen

Last name: Ali

Date of birth: 18 June 1987

City: Birmingham

Country: United Kingdom

Languages: English, Urdu, Punjabi

Job: Cricket player

> 1

Email: info@Mofans.cup.org

> 2

Father: Munir Ali
Brothers: Kadeer Ali, Omar Ali
Wife: Firoza Hossain
Son: Abu Bakr

> 3

Hobbies: reading, watching cricket, playing with my son

> 4

I'm Moeen Ali. I am from Birmingham in the United Kingdom. I speak three languages: English, Urdu and Punjabi. I am a cricket player. I have won many matches. My brothers also play cricket. Their names are Kadeer and Omar. My father is a cricket coach. He is from the UK. His father is from Pakistan. I like reading and watching cricket.

WHILE READING

3 Read the text on page 19 quickly. Write the words from the box in the gaps in the text.

> Contact information   My hobbies and interests
> My family   My life

4 Read the text again. Circle the correct words to make true sentences.

1 Moeen is from *Pakistan / the United Kingdom*.
2 Moeen's brothers play *football / cricket*.
3 Moeen's hobbies are *playing football and reading / watching cricket and reading*.
4 Moeen speaks *English / Arabic*.
5 Kadeer is Moeen's *brother / father*.
6 Moeen's email address is *info@Mofans.cup.org / Mofans@info.cup.org*.
7 His *wife / father* is a cricket coach.

5 Read the summary and circle the correct words.

> Moeen Ali is a [1] *cricket / football* player. He is from
> [2] *Birmingham / Manchester* in the United Kingdom.
> His date of birth is 18 June [3] *1987 / 1997*. He has two
> [4] *sisters / brothers*. His father is [5] *Abu Bakr / Munir Ali*.

DISCUSSION

6 Ask and answer the questions with a partner.

1 What is your date of birth?
2 Do you have any brothers or sisters?
3 What are your brothers' and sisters' names?
4 What languages do you speak?
5 What are your hobbies?

READING 2

PREPARING TO READ

1 Look at the text and photos on page 22. Then choose the correct answers.

1 The man in the photo is ...
  a at a shop.   b in his home.   c in a park.
2 The text is about a ...
  a farm.   b cricket player.   c very tall man.
3 The text is from a ...
  a book.   b magazine.   c website.

2 You are going to read an article about an unusual man. Read the sentences (1–8). Write the words in bold next to the correct definitions (a–h).

1 That is an **unusual** job! I have never heard of it.
2 I am a student at an English university. I **live** in London.
3 I am a teacher. I **work** in a school.
4 Andrea is **interested in** languages. She wants to learn Japanese.
5 I like to listen to **music**. I like the sound of the piano.
6 I **watch** TV at night. I watch cricket and other sports.
7 On a **normal** day, I go to work. Then I come home and eat dinner with my family.
8 My **family** is big. I have a mother, a father, four sisters and three brothers.

a _____ (n) a group of people related to each other, such as a mother, a father and their children
b _____ (adj) usual, ordinary and expected
c _____ (v) to have your home somewhere
d _____ (adj phr) wanting to learn more about something
e _____ (n) sounds that are made by playing instruments or singing
f _____ (adj) different and not usual, often in a way which is interesting or exciting
g _____ (v) to do a job, especially the job you do to get money
h _____ (v) to look at something for some time

PLUS

Sultan Kösen is a tall man.

A VERY tall man!

1 Sultan Kösen is from Turkey. He **lives** in Mardin in Turkey. He lives with his **family**. Sultan has a wife, three brothers and one sister.

2 Sultan is a farmer[1]. His hobby is **watching** TV. He is **interested in music**. His height[2] is **unusual**. He is 251 cm tall – that is very tall. Sultan is the tallest man in the world. His mother, brothers, sister and wife are **normal** height.

3 Sultan **works** on the farm. He has a tractor. His life is not easy. People look at him in the street. Normal clothes and shoes are too small. His clothes and shoes are very big.

4 Sultan speaks Turkish and English. He went to London, Paris and Madrid in Europe in 2010. He went to New York, Chicago and Los Angeles in the United States in 2011.

[1] **farmer** (n) someone who owns or works on a farm

[2] **height** (n) how tall or high something or someone is

tractor

WHILE READING

3 Read the text and circle the correct words in the profile below.

▪ PROFILE

First name: (1) *Sultan / Kösen*

Last name: (2) *Sultan / Kösen*

Country: (3) *Turkey / the United States*

City: (4) *Mardin / New York*

Family: (5) *three sisters and one brother / one sister
and three brothers*

Hobby: (6) *watching TV / working on a farm*

4 Read the text again. Write the correct words from the text in the gaps.

1 Sultan Kösen _____ from Turkey.

2 He _____ in Mardin in Turkey.

3 He lives with his _____ .

4 Sultan _____ a farmer.

5 His hobby is _____ TV.

6 Sultan _____ Turkish and English.

DISCUSSION

5 Work with a partner. Use information from Reading 1 and Reading 2 to
answer the following questions.

1 Sultan's life is not easy. Why?

2 What is Moeen interested in? What is Sultan interested in?

3 What can you learn from a profile?

4 Do you like reading profiles? Why / Why not?

FAMILY VOCABULARY

1 Write the nouns from the box in the correct columns in the table.

brother daughter grandfather mother uncle

family vocabulary	
male (man)	**female (woman)**
1 _____	grandmother
father	4 _____
son	5 _____
2 _____	sister
3 _____	aunt

NOUNS AND VERBS

Words for people, places or things are *nouns*. Words for states or actions are *verbs*. Sentences have nouns and verbs.

nouns: **Sultan** is a **farmer**. He lives in **Mardin**. He works on a **farm**.

verbs: Sultan **is** a farmer. He **lives** in Mardin. He **works** on a farm.

2 Read the sentences. Write the bold words in the correct columns in the table on page 25.

1 Moeen Ali's grandfather is from **Pakistan**.
2 Sultan Kösen **lives** on a farm.
3 Moeen Ali's brothers like **cricket**.
4 Sultan Kösen **works** in Turkey.
5 He **is** interested in music.
6 Moeen Ali **plays** with his son.
7 Sultan speaks two **languages**.

PLUS

nouns	verbs

Singular and plural nouns

Nouns are *singular* or *plural*. Singular means one. Plural means more than one. For most nouns, add -s at the end of the singular form to make the plural form.

singular nouns: Ray has one **brother**. His **brother** is a **farmer**.

plural nouns: Fernando has two **brothers**. His **brothers** are **farmers**.

Some plural nouns have irregular forms:

man ➡ **men**

woman ➡ **women**

person ➡ **people**

3 Read the sentences and circle the correct words.

1 My mother has four *sister / sisters*.
2 I have only one *aunt / aunts*.
3 I have a *grandfather / grandfathers* in Dubai.
4 My grandmother has two *son / sons* in Scotland.
5 She has five *brother / brothers*.

4 Read the sentences and write the words from the box in the gaps.

brothers   city   languages   lives   reads   sister

1 Moeen Ali _____ books.
2 Erika is my _____ . She lives with me.
3 She speaks two _____ : Arabic and English.
4 I have a sister and three _____ .
5 My grandfather _____ in Istanbul.
6 Rio de Janeiro is a big _____ . My mother works there.

 PLUS

WRITING

CRITICAL THINKING

At the end of this unit, you are going to write a profile. Look at this unit's writing task in the box below.

> Write a profile of your family.

 REMEMBER

1 Work with a partner. Ask and answer the questions about Sultan from Reading 2 on page 22.

1 What is Sultan's last name?
2 Where does Sultan live?
3 Who is in Sultan's family?
4 What is Sultan's job?

5 What are Sultan's hobbies?
6 What languages does Sultan speak?

SKILLS

Collecting information

Before you write, collect information. This information can come from your knowledge, books, the internet, people or other places. Use a table to record the information.

 APPLY

2 Use the table to write information about you.

first name	
last name	
date of birth	
city	
country	
family	
job	
hobbies	
languages	

3 Work with a partner and use your table. Ask your partner questions like the ones in Exercise 1. Then answer the questions about you.

GRAMMAR FOR WRITING

SUBJECT PRONOUNS

> *Subject pronouns* can replace nouns. Use subject pronouns before a verb.
> Subject pronouns are: *I, you, he, she, it, we* and *they.*

I am Min Lee. (Always use a capital letter for the pronoun *I*.)	I = Min Lee
You are my sister, Laura.	You = Laura
Thomas is 26. **He** is 26.	He = Thomas
Sarah is a student. **She** is a student.	She = Sarah
Busan is a city in South Korea. **It** is a big city.	It = Busan
Matt and I are brothers. **We** are brothers.	We = Matt and I
Mohammed and Yusuf, **you** are my friends.	you = Mohammed and Yusuf
Eduardo and Ana are from Colombia. **They** are from Colombia.	They = Eduardo and Ana

1 Work with a partner. Write the words from the box in the table.

> aunts   brother   daughter   father   grandfather
> grandmother   mother   sisters   sons   uncles

she	
he	
they	

2 Read the sentences and write the words from the box in the gaps.

> He   It   She   They

1 My sister is tall. _____ is 174 cm.
2 My aunts are Mexican. _____ are from Mexico City.
3 My uncle likes basketball. _____ plays every day.
4 Los Angeles is in California. _____ is a big city.

The verb *be* has three forms in the present simple: *am, is* and *are*. After *I*, use *am*. After *you, we* and *they*, use *are*. After *he, she* and *it*, use *is*.

<table>
<tr><th colspan="3">singular</th></tr>
<tr><th>subject</th><th>*be*</th><th></th></tr>
<tr><td>I</td><td>am</td><td rowspan="4">tall.
a student.</td></tr>
<tr><td>You</td><td>are</td></tr>
<tr><td>He
She
It</td><td>is</td></tr>
</table>

<table>
<tr><th colspan="3">plural</th></tr>
<tr><th>subject</th><th>*be*</th><th></th></tr>
<tr><td>We</td><td rowspan="3">are</td><td rowspan="3">from Turkey.
students.</td></tr>
<tr><td>You</td></tr>
<tr><td>They</td></tr>
</table>

Use *not* after *am / is / are* to make negative statements.

I **am not** from Busan.   He **is not** tall.   They **are not** farmers.

Contractions

Use contractions (short forms) in informal writing and in speaking.

singular	plural
I am → I'm you are → you're he is → he's she is → she's it is → it's	we are → we're you are → you're they are → they're

I'm from Riyadh.   She's from Beijing.   They're from Cairo.

Negative contractions

singular	plural
I am not → I'm not you are not → you **aren't** / you're not he is not → he **isn't** / he's not she is not → she **isn't** / she's not it is not → it **isn't** / it's not	we **aren't** / we're not you **aren't** / you're not they **aren't** / they're not

There are two negative forms.

He **is not** tall. = He **isn't** tall. = He's **not** tall.
We **are not** brothers. = We **aren't** brothers. = We're **not** brothers.

3 Read paragraphs A and B, and write *am*, *is* or *are* in the gaps.

My name (1)_____ Khalid.
I (2)_____ from Al Ain. I (3)_____
19. Al Ain (4)_____ in the United
Arab Emirates. My brother's name
(5)_____ Faisal. He (6)_____ older.
He (7)_____ 26. My father's name
(8)_____ Ali.

B

I (1)_____ Min Lee. I (2)_____
from Busan. Busan (3)_____ in South
Korea. I live with my mother, my father
and my sister. My mother and father
(4)_____ from Seoul. My sister's name
(5)_____ Hani. She (6)_____ 17.
She (7)_____ a student. Her hobbies
(8)_____ playing basketball and
watching TV.

4 Write *am not*, *is not* or *are not* in the gaps.

1 I _____ from Guangzhou. I am from Beijing.
2 Ana and Feride _____ sisters. They are friends.
3 Ahmed is from Jeddah. He _____ from Riyadh.
4 Daniella is from Mexico City. She _____ from Guadalajara.
5 My parents _____ from China. They are from South Korea.
6 We _____ farmers. We are doctors.

5 Correct five mistakes in the text below.

My name am Ibrihim. My family is from Tunisia. I have two
sisters and one brother. My sisters is in school in Tunis. They are
11 and 12. My brother is 22. He are a teacher in Spain. I live
with my brother. We is in Madrid. I are at university. I speak
Spanish, Arabic and English.

6 Rewrite the sentences. Use contractions.

1 I am from Tokyo.
_____

2 We are students in London.
_____

3 It is a big city.
_____

4 You are not tall.
_____

5 She is not a student.
_____

6 He is a teacher.
_____

7 You are students in my class.
_____

8 It is not a big school.
_____

9 We are not in Mexico.
_____

10 I am not at university.
_____

POSSESSIVE ADJECTIVES

Possessive adjectives show that someone owns or has something. They can also show family relationships. The possessive adjectives are: *my, your, his, her, its, our* and *their*.

Use possessive adjectives before a noun.

subject pronoun	possessive adjective	
I	my	I am from Turkey. **My** city is Istanbul.
you	your	You are from Egypt. **Your** school is in Alexandria.
she	her	Natalia is from Italy. **Her** father is from Rome.
he	his	Sultan lives in Mardin. **His** family is in Turkey.
it	its	Japan is a country in Asia. **Its** capital is Tokyo.
we	our	We have a big family. **Our** uncle is in Dubai.
they	their	Marta and Luis have a sister. **Their** sister is a teacher.

7 Read the sentences and write the words from the box in the gaps.

> Her   His   Its   My   Our   Their

1 I have two sisters. _____ names are Frances and Celia.
2 Jenny Fielding is from Miami. _____ father's name is David.
3 We go to school in London. _____ school is very big.
4 I have a brother and a sister. _____ sister's name is Andrea.
5 Moeen Ali is from the United Kingdom. _____ grandfather is from Pakistan.
6 I live in a big city. _____ name is Tokyo.

WRITING SIMPLE SENTENCES

A *simple sentence* has a subject and a verb. The sentence is about the subject. The verb comes after the subject.

subject   *verb*
noun: **Sultan** is from Turkey.

subject   *verb*
noun phrase: **His life** is not easy.

subject verb   *subject verb*
pronoun: **I** am from Beijing. **It** is a big city.

Begin the first word in a sentence with a capital letter (A, B, C). Put a full stop (.) at the end of the sentence.
He watches TV.

Remember: Sentences always have a subject and a verb.

subject   *verb*
✔ Moeen Ali plays cricket.

subject   *missing verb*
✘ Moeen Ali cricket.

1 Put the words in order to make simple sentences.

1 Zhong Shan / My grandfather's name / is / .

_____

2 is / He / 59 / .

_____

3 a doctor / He / is / .

_____

4 is from / He / Hong Kong / .

_____

5 two daughters / He / has / .

_____

6 my mother and father / lives with / He / .

_____

PLUS

2 Correct the mistakes in the simple sentences. Check for capital letters and full stops. Is there a subject and a verb in the sentence?

1 my name is Gustavo.

_____

2 i am from Ecuador

_____

3 i 19

_____

4 my father's name Marcus.

_____

5 she a teacher

_____

6 he has two sons.

_____

7 my brother's name is Paulo.

_____

8 is a doctor

_____

9 she in Canada

_____

10 Paulo's hobbies playing with his son and watching TV

_____

WRITING TASK

Write a profile of your family.

PLAN

1 Look back at your table in the Critical thinking section on page 26. Check your notes and add any new information to your profile, including information about your family. Think about:

- your family's names and ages
- the languages your family speaks
- your family's jobs
- your family's hobbies

2 Read the Task checklist on page 34 as you prepare your profile.

WRITE A FIRST DRAFT

3 Write sentences for your profile. Use the words in the table below and the information from your table in the Critical thinking section to help you.

A	B	C
I	am	a teacher.
My name My family	is	Hiro. from Kyoto.
My brothers and sisters My hobbies	are	students in London. watching TV and playing basketball.
I She He They We	live(s) with	my uncle. my mother and father.
	speak(s)	Japanese. Spanish. Turkish. Chinese. English. Arabic and English.

EDIT

4 Use the Task checklist to review your profile.

TASK CHECKLIST	✔
Make sure each sentence has a subject and a verb.	
Make sure each sentence begins with a capital letter and ends with a full stop.	
Use the correct form of *be* with subjects and subject pronouns.	
Use possessive adjectives (*my, his, her*) before a noun (*brother, sister, uncle*).	
Make sure people's names and places have capital letters.	
Make sure the personal pronouns *he* and *she* are before the verb *is*.	
Make sure the personal pronouns *we* and *they* are before the verb *are*.	

5 Make any necessary changes to your profile.

OBJECTIVES REVIEW

1 Check your learning objectives for this unit. Write *3, 2* or *1* for each objective.

3 = very well   2 = well   1 = not so well

I can ...

watch and understand a video about people who catch fish in different countries.   ‒‒‒‒‒

preview a text.   ‒‒‒‒‒

collect information.   ‒‒‒‒‒

use nouns and verbs.   ‒‒‒‒‒

use subject pronouns.   ‒‒‒‒‒

use the verb *be* (present simple).   ‒‒‒‒‒

use possessive adjectives.   ‒‒‒‒‒

write simple sentences.   ‒‒‒‒‒

write a profile.   ‒‒‒‒‒

2 Go to the *Unlock* Online Workbook for more practice with this unit's learning objectives.

UNLOCK ONLINE

WORDLIST

aunt (n)	grandfather (n)	music (n) ⊙
brother (n) ⊙	grandmother (n)	normal (adj) ⊙
city (n) ⊙	hobby (n)	sister (n) ⊙
country (n) ⊙	interested in (adj phr)	son (n) ⊙
date of birth (n)	job (n) ⊙	uncle (n)
daughter (n) ⊙	language (n) ⊙	unusual (adj) ⊙
family (n) ⊙	live (v) ⊙	watch (v) ⊙
father (n)	mother (n) ⊙	work (v) ⊙

⊙ = high-frequency words in the Cambridge Academic Corpus

LEARNING OBJECTIVES	IN THIS UNIT YOU WILL ...
Watch and listen	watch and understand a video about the taiga forest.
Reading skill	scan to find information.
Critical thinking	categorize information.
Grammar	use nouns and adjectives; use noun phrases; use prepositional phrases.
Academic writing skills	use correct word order; use correct punctuation.
Writing task	write about the weather.

UNL CK YOUR KNOWLEDGE

Look at the photo and ask and answer the questions with a partner.

1 Does this look like a nice time of year? Why / Why not?

2 Does this look like your country? Why / Why not?

3 What time of year do you like best? Why?

PLUS

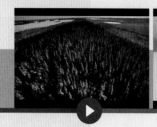   

PREPARING TO WATCH

ACTIVATING YOUR KNOWLEDGE

1 Work with a partner and answer the questions.

1 Which seasons do you have in your country?
2 Do you prefer hot and sunny weather or cold and snowy weather? Why?
3 Where in the world is it very cold?

PREDICTING CONTENT USING VISUALS

2 Look at the pictures from the video. Write *T* (true) or *F* (false) next to the statements. Correct the false statements.

_____ 1 This part of the Earth is warm.

_____

_____ 2 Part of the river is frozen.

_____

_____ 3 There is ice and snow on the trees.

_____

_____ 4 The trees die in the winter.

_____

GLOSSARY

temperature (n) how hot or cold something is, for example, 0 °C

river (n) a long natural area of water that goes across the land

fir trees / pine trees (n) trees with thin, hard green leaves that stay green all winter

forest (n) a large area with many trees growing closely together

freezing (adj) very cold

heavy snow (n phr) a lot of snow

WHILE WATCHING

3 ▶ Watch the video. Tick (✔) the statements that you hear.

1 ☐ The days grow short and cold.
2 ☐ Winter is hard here.
3 ☐ Water in the air, in rivers and in plants turns to ice.
4 ☐ All of the plants die.
5 ☐ During the winter, heavy snow covers the taiga.
6 ☐ Cold temperatures return in spring.

UNDERSTANDING
MAIN IDEAS

4 ▶ Watch again. Circle the correct answer.

1 Snow and cold temperatures move *north / south*.
2 Fir trees can live in very *warm / cold* temperatures.
3 The taiga forest has almost *20% / 30%* of all the trees on Earth.
4 Heavy *snow / rain* covers part of the taiga until the spring.

UNDERSTANDING
DETAIL

5 Read the sentences below and write the words from the box in the gaps.

difficult   flowers   near   winter

1 The _____ is very long in the taiga forest.
2 The taiga forest is _____ the North Pole.
3 Living in the taiga forest is _____ in winter.
4 _____ do not grow in winter in the taiga forest.

MAKING INFERENCES

DISCUSSION

6 Ask and answer the questions with a partner.

1 Do you think it is easy for people to live in the taiga forest?
Why / Why not?
2 How long do you think winter is in the taiga forest?
3 Which season is the longest in your country?
4 What things do you take with you when you go to a cold place?

READING

PREPARING TO READ

UNDERSTANDING KEY VOCABULARY

1 You are going to read an article about a city with cold weather. Look at the words in bold. Match sentences 1–3 with a–c.

1 Italy is **warm**.	a In winter, the temperatures are freezing.
2 Sweden is **cold**.	b In summer, everyone enjoys the sun.
3 **Spring** is before **summer**.	c **Autumn** is before **winter**.

2 Match the words (1–7) to the correct numbers (a–g).

1	eleven	a	8
2	eighteen	b	18
3	twenty-one	c	6
4	forty-two	d	42
5	fifty	e	21
6	eight	f	11
7	six	g	50

USING YOUR KNOWLEDGE

3 Look at the temperatures in the box. Ask and answer the questions with a partner.

0 °C   +16 °C   +35 °C

1 Which temperature do you like best? Why?
2 What clothes do people wear outside for each temperature?
3 What is the temperature in summer where you live? What is the temperature in winter?

4 Look at the graph, photographs and heading in the article on page 41. Write *T* (true) or *F* (false) next to the statements. Correct the false statements.

_____ 1 Yakutsk is a city.

_____

_____ 2 Winter is very cold in Yakutsk.

_____

_____ 3 Summer is very cold in Yakutsk.

_____

_____ 4 Svetlana has a café in Moscow.

_____

THE COLDEST CITY IN THE WORLD

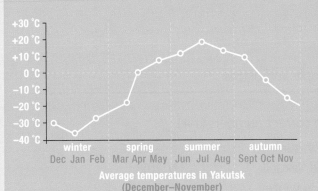

Average temperatures in Yakutsk
(December–November)

+30 °C			
+20 °C			
+10 °C			
0 °C			
–10 °C			
–20 °C			
–30 °C			
–40 °C			
winter	**spring**	**summer**	**autumn**
Dec Jan Feb	Mar Apr May	Jun Jul Aug	Sept Oct Nov

ice skating

skiing

1 The temperature in your freezer is **cold**. It is about –18 °C. The city of Yakutsk in Russia is colder than your freezer. In **winter**, the average temperature[1] is –42 °C!

2 In 2018, I visited Yakutsk. Why? Because I wanted to see the coldest city in the world. I wanted to meet the people of Yakutsk.

Svetlana has a warm café in a cold city.

3 'Life is difficult in winter,' says Svetlana, 'but we're not sad.' Svetlana is the manager of a café[2] in Yakutsk. She has two children. Her son Pavel is 11. Her daughter Daria is 5.

4 'The average temperature in winter is –42 °C. Some winters are colder. At –55 °C, the schools are closed. Daria and Pavel are happy,' Svetlana says.

5 People in Yakutsk like sport[3]. In **spring** and **autumn**, the average temperature is –21 °C. They go skiing and ice skating. In **summer**, it is **warm**. The average temperature is +20 °C. People take food and drinks to eat outside.

[1]**average temperature** (n phr) how hot or cold a place usually is
[2]**café** (n) a small restaurant where you can buy drinks and food
[3]**sport** (n) a game or activity which people do to keep healthy or for fun

WHILE READING

Scanning to find information

Scanning means looking for information. When we scan, we do not read every word in a text. We can scan for information such as:

- numbers
- names of people
- names of places

Look for capital letters to find people and places.

5 Match the facts (1–6) to the correct numbers (a–f).

1	the average temperature in summer	**a**	−42 °C
2	the year the writer visited Yakutsk	**b**	2018
3	the average temperature in winter	**c**	5
4	Daria's age	**d**	−55 °C
5	the average temperature in spring and autumn	**e**	−21 °C
		f	+20 °C
6	the temperature when schools are closed		

6 Write the words from the box in the gaps to complete the summary of the text.

> cold   spring   Svetlana   warm   Yakutsk

> The text is about (1)_____ and her family. They live in the city of (2)_____ in Russia. Winters are very (3)_____ . Sometimes school is closed. In (4)_____ and autumn, people go skiing and ice skating. In summer, it is (5)_____ .

DISCUSSION

7 Ask and answer the questions with a partner.

1 Do you want to live in Yakutsk? Why / Why not?
2 When is a good time to visit Yakutsk? Why?
3 What do you do in cold temperatures?

READING 2

PREPARING TO READ

USING YOUR
KNOWLEDGE

1 Work with a partner. Talk about winter, spring, summer and autumn in your city or town. Do you have all four seasons? What months are in each season?

months	
January	July
February	August
March	September
April	October
May	November
June	December

PREVIEWING

2 Look at Texts A, B and C on page 44. Choose the correct answers (a–c) to the questions (1–3).

1 Where are the texts from?
   a a book   **b** a magazine   **c** a website
2 Which text is about the weather in Cuba now?
   a Text A   **b** Text B   **c** Text C
3 Which texts are about typical weather in Cuba?
   a Texts A and B   **b** Texts B and C   **c** Texts A and C

UNDERSTANDING
KEY VOCABULARY

3 You are going to read about the weather in Cuba. Read the definitions in the box. Then write the words from the box in the gaps in 1–4.

> **dry** (adj) with very little or no rain
> **rainfall** (n) the amount of rain that falls in one place
> **season** (n) one of the four parts of the year: winter, spring, summer or autumn
> **climate** (n) the weather that a place usually has

1 The _____ in spring is often high. It is good for the plants.
2 Summer is my favourite _____ . I like warm temperatures.
3 The desert is very _____ . Little rain falls there.
4 The _____ in the desert is hot and dry.

4 Write the words from the box in the gaps in Text A.

| cloudy | sunny | rainy | windy |

A

CUBA WEATHER   HOME | <u>WEATHER</u> | CUBAN CLIMATE | WEATHER AVERAGES

TODAY | TOMORROW | 5 DAY | MONTHLY

TODAY

(1) _____

+29 °C

MONDAY

cloudy and
(2) _____

+28 °C

TUESDAY

(3) _____
and cloudy

+26 °C

WEDNESDAY

sunny and
(4) _____

+29 °C

THURSDAY

sunny

+31 °C

B

CUBA WEATHER   HOME | WEATHER | <u>CUBAN CLIMATE</u> | WEATHER AVERAGE

1 Cuba is in the Caribbean. The **climate** in Cuba is good. It has two **seasons**: the **dry** season and the **rainy** season. The dry season and the rainy season each last for six months.

2 The dry season is from November to April. The average temperatures are between +22 °C and +25 °C in the dry season. The average **rainfall** is 62 mm in the dry season. It is **windy** and **sunny** in the dry season.

3 The rainy season is from May to October. In the rainy season, the average temperatures are between +26 °C and +28 °C. The average rainfall in the rainy season is 146 mm. It is often **cloudy**.

4 The best time to visit Cuba is April or May.

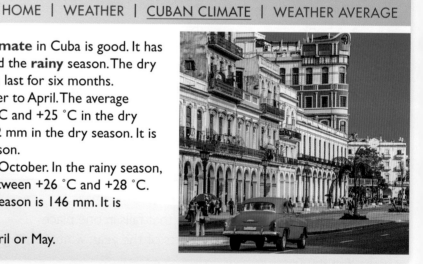

C

CUBA WEATHER   HOME | WEATHER | CUBAN CLIMATE | <u>WEATHER AVERAGES</u>

SEASON (MONTHS)	AVERAGE TEMPERATURE	AVERAGE RAINFALL	AVERAGE WIND SPEED
Dry (Nov–Apr)	+23 °C	62 mm	8 kph
Rainy (May–Oct)	+27 °C	146 mm	15 kph

WHILE READING

5 Read the three texts (A–C) quickly. Match the facts (1–6) to the correct numbers (a–f).

1 number of months in the dry season   a +26
2 average temperatures (°C) in the dry season   b +31
3 average rainfall (mm) in the dry season   c +23
4 average rainfall (mm) in the rainy season   d 146
5 temperature (°C) on Tuesday   e 6
6 temperature (°C) on Thursday   f 62

6 Look at Text B again. Take notes on the seasons in the table.

dry season	rainy season

DISCUSSION

7 Work with a partner. Use ideas from Reading 1 and Reading 2 to answer the questions.

1 When is a good time to visit Cuba? Why do you think those months are good?
2 What are the seasons in Cuba?
3 Where can you find facts about the climate in a country?
4 Why do people want to know about the weather and climate of a place?

NOUNS AND ADJECTIVES

GRAMMAR

Words for people, places or things are *nouns*. Words that describe people, places and things are *adjectives*.

We write adjectives before a noun.

good climate, **cold** winter, **happy** child

Adjectives always go after *is / are* (*not*).

Summer is **nice**.

Ice skating and skiing are **popular** in my country.

The rainy season is not **dry**.

PLUS

1 Match the adjectives (1–7) with their opposites (a–g).

1	difficult	**a**	warm
2	cold	**b**	dry
3	sunny	**c**	hot
4	cool	**d**	cloudy
5	rainy	**e**	unpopular
6	popular	**f**	easy
7	happy	**g**	sad

2 Underline the nouns and circle the adjectives in the sentences.

1 The café is warm.
2 October is rainy.
3 The climate is good.
4 Summers are hot.
5 Winters are cold.

3 Read the sentences. Write the words from the box in the gaps.

cloudy   cold   difficult   happy   sunny

1 In Yakutsk, life is _____ in winter.
2 The children are _____ . There is no school today.
3 It is warm and _____ today.
4 The winter is _____ in Yakutsk.
5 The rainy season is _____ . You do not see the sun for days.

NOUN PHRASES

GRAMMAR

A *noun phrase* is a noun and another word that describes or defines the noun. When an adjective comes before a noun, it is part of a noun phrase.

noun phrases: Cuba has **a good climate**. **The average rainfall** is 62 mm.

Use *has* to show that the noun phrase belongs to the subject.
Cuba **has** a dry season.

Use *be* to link the noun phrase with a word or phrase that describes it.
The rainy season **is** from May to October.

4 Make a noun phrase from the bold words in each sentence. Write it in the gaps to make a new sentence.

 1 Yakutsk's **winters** are **cold**.
 Yakutsk has _____ _____ .
 2 The **season** is **dry** from November to April.
 The _____ _____ is from November to April.
 3 In the rainy season, the **rainfall** is **high**.
 The rainy season has _____ _____ .
 4 **Summers** are **warm** in Yakutsk.
 Yakutsk has _____ _____ .

PLUS

5 Work with a partner. Correct the mistakes in the sentences. Check the adjectives in the noun phrases and after the verbs *be* and *have*.

 1 Cuba has a season rainy.

 _____

 2 Yakutsk has a autumn cold.

 _____

 3 In summer, we have weather sunny.

 _____

 4 The dry season windy is.

 _____

 5 In spring, the rainfall high is.

 _____

WRITING

At the end of this unit, you are going to write about the weather. Look at this unit's writing task in the box below.

> Write about the weather in your city or town.

SKILLS

Categorizing information

After you collect information, the next step is to categorize it, or put the information in groups. Look at the headings in the table. A table is a good way to categorize information. It is easy to see facts and numbers.

season	months	average temperature
spring	March, April, May	+21 °C

APPLY

1 Complete the table below about Yakutsk. Use information from the text and graph on page 41.

season	months	average temperature
winter		
	March, April and May	
		−21 °C

2 Work with a partner. Look at the table in Exercise 1 on page 48. Ask and answer the questions.

1 Is Yakutsk cold in February?
2 Is Yakutsk warm in August?
3 What is the weather like in April?
4 When is autumn?
5 Is spring warm or cold?

3 Think of your own city or town. Circle the seasons there.

| dry season   autumn   rainy season   spring   summer   winter |

4 Create a table for the seasons in your city or town. If you don't know the information, write what you think it is.

season	months	average temperature

5 Compare your answers with a partner. Then use the internet to check and correct your information.

GRAMMAR FOR WRITING

PREPOSITIONAL PHRASES

The words *about*, *in*, *from*, *between* and *for* are examples of *prepositions*. A *prepositional phrase* is a preposition + a noun. Use prepositional phrases to say where, when and how long, and to give an estimate or range.

where: Svetlana is **from Yakutsk**. Yakutsk is **in Russia**.

when: It is warm **in summer**. It is cold **in January**.

how long: The rainy season lasts **for six months**. The rainy season lasts **from May to October**.

estimate or range: It is **about −18 °C**. The dry season lasts **about six months**. The average temperatures are **between +22 °C and +25 °C**.

1 Read the sentences. Write the prepositions from the box in the gaps. You can use one preposition more than once.

> about   between   for   in

1 People _____ Yakutsk like sport.
2 It is windy _____ the dry season in Cuba.
3 The average temperatures are _____ +26 °C and +28 °C in the dry season.
4 The temperature _____ your freezer is _____ −18 °C.
5 Winter lasts _____ three months in Yakutsk.

2 Answer the questions. Use the correct prepositions in your answers.

1 Where are you from?

_____

2 When is it warm in your city?

_____

3 How long is the winter in your country?

_____

4 What is the average temperature in May in your city?

_____

5 When is the weather nice in your city?

_____

Prepositional phrases and punctuation

When a prepositional phrase begins a sentence, use a comma after it.

In the rainy season, the average temperatures are between +26 °C and +28 °C.

In spring and autumn, the average temperature is −21 °C.

3 Circle the prepositional phrase in the sentences.

1 In the dry season, the average temperatures are between +26 °C and +28 °C.

2 The average temperatures are between +26 °C and +28 °C in the dry season.

4 Look at the sentences in Exercise 3. Answer the questions.

1 Which sentence has a comma after the prepositional phrase?
_____

2 What preposition is used to give a range in temperatures? _____

5 Write the prepositional phrases from the box in the gaps. Add commas if necessary.

in July   in the dry season   in the rainy season

1 It is hot in Cuba _____ .
2 _____ the average rainfall is 146 mm.
3 The average rainfall is 62 mm _____ .

6 Add five commas to the text.

Dubai is a great place to visit. From November to March many people go to the beach. The weather is good. In these months the temperatures are between +24 °C and +35 °C. From January to March Dubai has a rainy season, but it does not rain a lot. Summer is from April to October. In summer Dubai is very hot. People do not go outside. In this season the temperatures are too high.

7 Put the words in order to make sentences. Remember to use a comma if a prepositional phrase begins the sentence.

1 windy / October / , / is / it / In / .

_____

2 weather / good / summer / is / The / in / .

_____

3 Cuba / climate / good / the / is / In / , / .

_____

4 the average / , / 34 mm / In / autumn / rainfall / is / .

_____

5 Yakutsk / The / are / cold / winters / in / .

_____

6 in / summer / is / The average temperature / +20 °C /.

_____

7 the dry season / 62 mm / In / , / average rainfall / is / the / .

_____

ACADEMIC WRITING SKILLS

WORD ORDER

Subject–verb–noun (phrase) / adjective

A sentence is about a *subject*. The subject is a pronoun, a noun or a noun phrase. Write the *verb* after the *subject* in a sentence. Write a noun, a noun phrase or an adjective after the verb *be*.

Noun or noun phrase: Svetlana is **the manager**. She is **the mother of two children**.

Adjective: Winter is **cold**. Life is **difficult**.

1 Circle the option that is true for you or your country.

   1 It *is / is not* cold in December.
   2 Skiing *is / is not* popular in my country.
   3 I am *happy / sad in spring*.
   4 I think the weather in my country is *good / bad*.
   5 It is *rainy / sunny* in August.
   6 It is *warm / cold* in November.
   7 The summer *is / is not* dry in my country.

2 Put the words in order to make sentences.

   1 is / in / Russia / Ice skating / popular / .

     _____

   2 are / two seasons / There / in Cuba / .

     _____

   3 rainy / is / It / in April / .

     _____

   4 hot / is / in Cuba / It / .

     _____

   5 are / warm / The summers / .

     _____

   6 dry / in August / is / It / .

     _____

   7 windy / it / In winter, / is / .

     _____

PLUS

PUNCTUATION

Capital letters

For the following types of words, the first letter is always a capital letter.

names of months: April, May, June

names of days: Monday, Tuesday, Wednesday

nationalities: Mexican, Egyptian, Korean

names of people: Juanna, Luis, Rodrigo

names of places: Turkey, Cairo, New York

Commas

Commas separate parts of a sentence or things in a list. Use a comma:
- after a prepositional phrase at the beginning of a sentence
- when listing three or more items

In winter, we go skiing.

In summer, we go swimming.

It is going to be windy on Monday, Wednesday, Thursday and Saturday.

We do not usually use a comma before *and*.

3 Add commas to the items in the lists.

1 It is spring in March April and May.
2 It rains in spring summer and autumn.
3 The coldest months are December January and February.
4 The warmest months are June July and August.

4 Correct the punctuation in the sentences. Add capital letters, commas and full stops.

1 in january the weather is cold in russia

_____

2 the average temperature is +21 °C in july

_____

3 in the rainy season the average rainfall is 146 mm in cuba

_____

4 the weather is sunny in summer

_____

5 in dubai august is a hot month

_____

WRITING TASK

Write about the weather in your city or town.

PLAN

1 Look back at your table in the Critical thinking section on page 49. Check your notes and add any new information you want to include.

2 Read the Task checklist on page 56 as you prepare your sentences.

WRITE A FIRST DRAFT

3 Write information about your city or town in the gaps below.

_____ (city or town) is in _____ (country). _____ (city or town) has _____ (number) seasons. The seasons are _____ .

4 Write sentences about your city.

1 Write a sentence about the weather in one season. (It is windy / cold / rainy.)

_____

2 Say which months the season is in (April / May).

_____

3 Write a sentence about the average temperatures in this season.

_____

4 Write a sentence about the weather in another season. (It is windy / cold / rainy.)

_____

5 Write a sentence about the average temperatures in this season.

_____

EDIT

5 Use the Task checklist to review your sentences.

TASK CHECKLIST	✔
Use adjectives before a noun or after the verb *be*.	
Use prepositional phrases to tell where, when or how long, or to give an estimate or range.	
Use commas after prepositional phrases which begin a sentence and for items in a list.	
Capitalize the beginning of a sentence and names of months, days, people, nationalities and places.	

6 Make any necessary changes to your sentences.

OBJECTIVES REVIEW

1 Check your learning objectives for this unit. Write *3*, *2* or *1* for each objective.

3 = very well   2 = well   1 = not so well

I can ...

watch and understand a video about the taiga forest. _____

scan to find information. _____

categorize information. _____

use nouns and adjectives. _____

use noun phrases. _____

use prepositional phrases. _____

use correct word order. _____

use correct punctuation. _____

write about the weather. _____

2 Go to the *Unlock* Online Workbook for more practice with this unit's learning objectives.

WORDLIST		
autumn (n) ⊙	rainfall (n) ⊙	sunny (adj)
climate (n) ⊙	rainy (adj)	warm (adj) ⊙
cloudy (adj)	season (n) ⊙	windy (adj)
cold (adj) ⊙	spring (n) ⊙	winter (n) ⊙
dry (adj) ⊙	summer (n) ⊙	

⊙ = high-frequency words in the Cambridge Academic Corpus

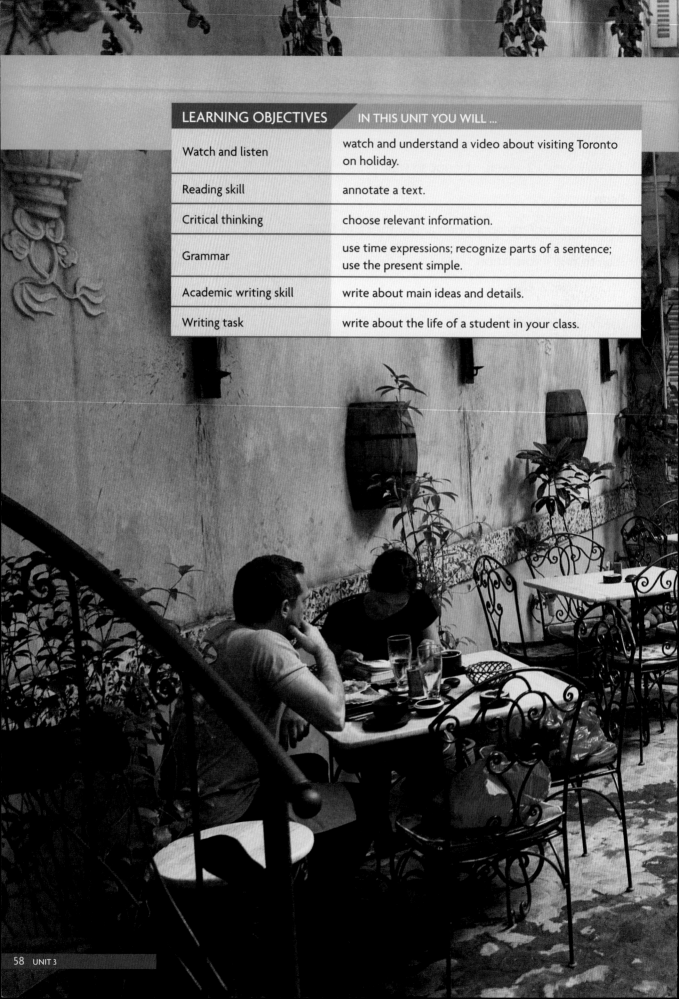

LEARNING OBJECTIVES	IN THIS UNIT YOU WILL ...
Watch and listen	watch and understand a video about visiting Toronto on holiday.
Reading skill	annotate a text.
Critical thinking	choose relevant information.
Grammar	use time expressions; recognize parts of a sentence; use the present simple.
Academic writing skill	write about main ideas and details.
Writing task	write about the life of a student in your class.

UNLOCK YOUR KNOWLEDGE

1 Look at the photo and ask and answer the questions with a partner.
Use the names of places from the box to help you.

| café   library   park |

1 Where are the people?
2 What are they doing?
3 Where do you study with friends? Why?
4 Where do you go with friends for fun? Why?

PLUS

PREPARING TO WATCH

ACTIVATING YOUR
KNOWLEDGE

1 Work with a partner and answer the questions.

1 Where is your favourite place to go on holiday? Why?
2 What do you like to do when you travel?
3 Do you enjoy activities that are a little bit dangerous? Why / Why not?
Talk about a dangerous activity that you enjoy / don't enjoy.

PREDICTING
CONTENT FROM
VISUALS

2 Look at the pictures from the video. Put the words in order to make a sentence.

1 the city from / the top of the CN tower / You can see / .

_____

2 of Lake Ontario / Toronto is / on the shore / .

_____

3 the main pod of the tower / This is / that people visit / .

_____

4 Five people are walking / of the CN Tower / on the outside / .

_____

GLOSSARY

popular (adj) something (or someone) that many people like
pod (n) a small, usually round, building
border (n) a line between two countries
brave (adj) not afraid

WHILE WATCHING

3 ▶ Watch the video. Tick (✔) the true sentences.

UNDERSTANDING
MAIN IDEAS

☐ 1 The CN Tower is Canada's most popular tourist attraction.
☐ 2 The CN Tower is the tallest building in Toronto.
☐ 3 The CN Tower was built to mark Canada's 100th birthday.
☐ 4 You can see the city and lake from several different places in the CN Tower.
☐ 5 The Glass Floor is on the same level as the main pod.
☐ 6 You can walk on the outside of the CN Tower.

4 ▶ Watch again. Complete the sentences with numbers from the box.

UNDERSTANDING
DETAIL

| 360 | 160 | 116 | 1976 |

1 The CN Tower opened in _____ .
2 From the LookOut level, there is a _____-degree view of the city and Lake Ontario.
3 Niagara Falls is _____ km from the centre of Toronto.
4 The EdgeWalk is _____ floors above the ground.

5 Match the sentence halves.

MAKING INFERENCES

1 The main job of the CN Tower is
2 You can see a view of the city
3 Niagara Falls is
4 The EdgeWalk is

a from different levels of the CN Tower.
b very exciting.
c communication.
d far from the CN Tower.

DISCUSSION

6 Work with a partner and answer the questions.

1 Which part of the CN Tower would you like to visit – the LookOut level, the Glass Floor or the SkyPod? Give reasons for your answer.
2 What place do people visit on holiday in your city? Describe it.
3 Have you visited a tall tower in another city? Describe what you saw.

READING

PREPARING TO READ

USING YOUR
KNOWLEDGE

PREVIEWING

UNDERSTANDING
KEY VOCABULARY

1 Ask and answer the questions with a partner.

1 Imagine you do not have a smartphone or TV. What do you do? How do you spend your time?

2 Imagine there are no supermarkets or restaurants. What do you eat?

2 Which things in the box can you see in the photos on page 63? Circle the words. Use a dictionary to help you.

> a writer   a hunter   a jungle   a tree house
> a TV   a website   a watch

3 You are going to read about a book that shows you a different way of life. Read the sentences (1–8). Write the words or phrases in bold next to the correct definitions (a–h).

1 I do not like to wake up early. I **get up** around 10:00 am.
2 I like to **cook** my food at home, but many of my friends eat at restaurants.
3 Before I go to work, I have coffee and toast for **breakfast** every morning.
4 I usually eat **lunch** at my desk at work. I usually have a salad or soup.
5 I eat **dinner** after work. Sometimes, I eat with friends at a restaurant.
6 I often **travel** to China and Japan for my work.
7 I **meet** a lot of people in my job. I really enjoy talking with new people.
8 I **swim** every Saturday. I have lessons at a pool near my house.

a _____ (n) the food you eat at the end of the day
b _____ (phr v) to leave your bed after sleeping
c _____ (v) to see and speak to someone for the first time
d _____ (n) the food you eat in the morning after you wake up
e _____ (v) to move through water by moving your body
f _____ (v) to prepare food by heating it
g _____ (n) the food you eat in the middle of the day
h _____ (v) to go from one place to another, usually over a long distance

Meet the Kombai

Can you imagine your life with no smartphones or TV? With no cars or supermarkets? Can you imagine life in a tree house?

1 In her book, *A Life in the Trees*, journalist[1] Rebecca Moore **travels** 15,000 kilometres (km) from London to Papua New Guinea. In Papua New Guinea, Rebecca **meets** the Kombai people. She talks about their lives in the jungle.

2 Moore lived with the Kombai women and children for three months. Kombai life is very different. The Kombai people have no watches[2] and no cars. There is no school for the children. Parents[3] teach their children to **cook**, hunt and **swim**.

3 The Kombai **get up** every morning at sunrise. Kombai men hunt in the jungle. They can hunt for 12 hours. They also cut down sago palms. This tree is important. The women cook the inside of the tree. The Kombai people eat this food for **breakfast**, **lunch** and **dinner**.

4 The most important part of Kombai life is building their tree houses. The men, women and children all help build tree houses. Each house is 20 metres (m) high. The stories in this book show the Kombai people's lives in the trees.

Kombai tree house

'**Buy this book!**'
Jeffrey Rost,
Lifestyle

'**It has amazing photographs on every page.**'
Simon Higgins,
New Look

woman preparing a sago palm

Kombai hunter

[1]**journalist** (n) someone whose job is to write articles for newspapers, magazines, etc.
[2]**watches** (n) small clocks on a strap that you wear on your arm
[3]**parents** (n) mother and father

WHILE READING

READING FOR
MAIN IDEAS

4 Read the text on page 63. Then match the sentence halves to create complete sentences about the text.

1 In Papua New Guinea, Rebecca meets   a the sago palm.
2 The Kombai women cook   b the Kombai people.
3 The Kombai people have   c build tree houses.
4 The men, women and children help to   d a different life.

5 Read the text again to check your answers.

SCANNING TO FIND
INFORMATION

6 Scan the text for the information in the table. Tick (✔) the person or people that do each action. There may be more than one answer. The first one has been done as an example.

	Rebecca Moore	Kombai men	Kombai women	Kombai children
1 hunt in the jungle		✔		
2 travel 15,000 km				
3 cook sago palms				
4 eat sago palms				
5 have no cars				
6 teach children to hunt, cook and swim				
7 build tree houses				
8 tell the story of the Kombai way of life				

DISCUSSION

7 Ask and answer the questions with a partner.

1 Why do you think the Kombai live in tree houses?
2 What do the Kombai people teach their children? Why?
3 The Kombai people eat sago palms three times a day. What is good and bad about eating the same food all the time?

PREPARING TO READ

1 Read the sentences (1–8). Choose the best definition (a or b) for the words in bold.

1 After lunch, I like to go for a walk in the **afternoon**.
  a the time between 12 pm and 6 pm
  b something you eat for lunch

2 I am very **busy** at university. I take many courses.
  a having a lot of friends
  b having a lot of things to do

3 My **timetable** is the same every day. I work and then go to school.
  a a place where you work to make money
  b a list or plan to show when you do things

4 I get up at 6 am every **morning**. I make coffee and eat breakfast.
  a the time between 5 am and 12 pm
  b the place where you make food

5 I **relax** after work. I watch TV.
  a to become calm and comfortable
  b to have many things to do

6 In the **evening**, I do my homework and read a book before bed.
  a a place you go to relax
  b the time between 6 pm and 11 pm

7 I have school on **weekdays**. I have to get up early.
  a the five days of the week when many people work
  b the two days of the week when many people do not work

8 At the **weekend**, I go cycling. I have fun with friends.
  a the two days of the week when many people do not work
  b the five days of the week when many people work

2 In your country, what days are weekdays? What days are weekends? List the things you do on weekdays and weekends. Compare your list with a partner.

Weekdays: _____ , _____ , _____ , _____ ,
_____

Things I do on weekdays:
_____
_____

Weekends: _____ , _____
Things I do at weekends:
_____
_____

3 Write the bold words from Exercise 1 in the correct columns in the table.

noun	verb	adjective	part of the day	part of the week

PREVIEWING

4 Look at the timetable below and the text on page 67. Write *T* (true) or *F* (false) next to the statements. Correct the false statements.

_____ **1** The timetable is for an Engineering student.

_____ **2** The timetable and the text are from a website.

_____ **3** The text and the timetable are about Abdullah Taha.

_____ **4** Abdullah's weekend is on Saturday and Sunday.

Name of student: _Abdullah Taha_   **Department:** _Engineering_

morning	Sun	Mon	Tue	Wed	Thur	Fri	Sat
8–9 am	Physics 101 lecture	Physics seminar	Physics 101 lecture	Physics 101	Physics 101 lecture		
9:15–10:15 am	Maths 121	Maths 121 lecture	Maths 121	Maths 121 lecture	Maths 121 seminar		
10:30–11:30 am	Engineering 122 lecture	Engineering 122 seminar	Engineering 122 lecture	Engineering 122	Engineering 122 lecture		

afternoon	Sun	Mon	Tue	Wed	Thur	Fri	Sat
12:30–1:30 pm	Study group						
2–3 pm		English 101	Library	English 101	Arab History 123 lecture		

evening	Sun	Mon	Tue	Wed	Thur	Fri	Sat
5–7 pm	Library	Library	Library	Library	Relax with friends		
7–10 pm	Library	Library	Camera Club	Go to the gym	Relax with friends		

Abdullah Taha

1 Abdullah Taha is a student in my class. He has a busy **timetable**. Abdullah studies Engineering[1] at Cairo University. Abdullah takes five courses. They are Physics[2], Maths, English, Engineering and Arab History[3]. His favourite subjects are Physics and Maths.

2 Abdullah is a **busy** student. He gets up at 6 am every **weekday**. He studies every evening. He has many classes, seminars and lectures every week.

3 Abdullah has three classes every **morning**. He has Physics from 8 am to 9 am, Maths from 9:15 am to 10:15 am and Engineering from 10:30 am to 11:30 am.

4 On Sunday, he meets his study group. His study group is from 12:30 pm to 1:30 pm. On Monday and Wednesday, he has English. His English class is from 2 pm to 3 pm. On Thursday **afternoon**, he has Arab History from 2 pm to 3 pm.

5 In the **evening**, Abdullah studies in the library. In his free time, Abdullah **relaxes** with friends. Sometimes, Abdullah goes to the cinema. Abdullah likes taking photographs. He is in the university Camera Club.

6 Abdullah says, 'My university life is very busy. I have a lot of exams and projects, but I always have time to relax with friends and family, especially at the **weekend**.'

[1]**Engineering** (n) the study of designing and building buildings, bridges, roads, etc.
[2]**Physics** (n) the scientific study of natural forces, such as energy, heat, light, etc.
[3]**History** (n) the study of events in the past

Annotating a text

When you *annotate*, you mark the text. For example, you can underline key words. Key words are the words or phrases which give the important information in the text. Look at the underlined words in the paragraph below. The reader has underlined the key words which give the most important information and details.

SKILLS

In her book, *A Life in the Trees*, journalist <u>Rebecca Moore</u> travels 15,000 km from London to Papua New Guinea. In Papua New Guinea, Rebecca <u>meets the Kombai people</u>. She tells about their <u>lives in the jungle</u>.

ANNOTATING

5 Read the text about Abdullah on page 67 again. Underline two or three key words or phrases in each paragraph. Then compare your key words with a partner. What is the important information? Take notes.

SCANNING TO FIND INFORMATION

6 Use the text and your notes from Exercise 5. Circle the correct key words to make true sentences about Abdullah.

1 Abdullah relaxes with friends *every evening / on Thursday evening*.
2 He is a student in *Cairo / Riyadh*.
3 He says that his life is *busy / quiet*.
4 He has *three / five* classes every morning.
5 He goes to the *Camera Club / gym* on Tuesday evening.
6 He studies Maths every *morning / afternoon*.
7 He gets up *late / early*.
8 He takes *three / five* courses at the university.
9 He has an Arab History class on *Tuesday / Thursday*.
10 He studies in the Department of *Engineering / English*.

DISCUSSION

SYNTHESIZING

7 Work with a partner. Use ideas from Reading 1 and Reading 2. Ask and answer the questions below.

1 When does Abdullah relax? What does he do to relax?
2 When do you relax? What do you do to relax?
3 Compare your life to the Kombai people and to Abdullah. What is the same? What is different?
4 Think about the things Abdullah and the Kombai people do. Which things do you like? Do you do them? Why / Why not?

⊙ LANGUAGE DEVELOPMENT

COLLOCATIONS FOR FREE-TIME ACTIVITIES

VOCABULARY

A pair or small group of words that are often used together is a *collocation*. One type of collocation is a verb + a noun or a noun phrase.

sentence	collocation (verb + noun or noun phrase)
I **have breakfast**.	have + breakfast
Hiroki and Ken **play video games**.	play + video games
Abdullah **studies English**.	studies + English

Another type of collocation is a verb + a prepositional phrase.

sentence	collocation (verb + prepositional phrase)
Abdullah **goes to the gym**.	goes + to the gym
Abdullah **studies in the library**.	studies + in the library
Abdullah **relaxes with friends**.	relaxes + with friends

1 Match the sentence halves.

1	Eun Jung **studies**	a	**coffee** before work.
2	Asif **gets up**	b	**Physics** at Cambridge University.
3	Melody and Ginger **take**	c	**at 6 am**.
4	In the morning, **I have**	d	**to the gym** every Saturday.
5	My friends **go**	e	**the bus** every morning.

2 Read the sentences and write the verbs from the box in the gaps.

> do   cooks   eats   go   have   meets   relax   take

1 Abdullah _____ **with** his study group on Sundays.
2 I _____ **the bus** to university every morning.
3 You _____ **to the gym** every day.
4 Melody and Ginger _____ **breakfast** at 7 am!
5 Li Mei _____ **her lunch** in the café.
6 Sandra and Andreia _____ **with friends** in the evening.
7 My sister _____ **dinner** for my family.
8 You _____ **your homework** in the evening.

PLUS

VOCABULARY FOR STUDY

3 Read the names of the subjects. Tick (✔) in the correct box. Use the glossary on page 192 to help you.

subject	Arts and Humanities	Business	Science	Languages
Maths			✔	
Physics				
Literature				
English				
Economics				
Biology				
History				
Management				
Arabic				
Geography				
Chemistry				
Art				

4 Check your answers with a partner. Then ask and answer the questions.

1 Which of the subjects in the table do you study?
2 Which do you enjoy?
3 Do you know any other subjects for each group?

5 Put the letters in the correct order to make the names of subjects.

1 ogypherag   G _____
2 snegihl   E _____
3 siphcsy   P _____
4 miechtyrs   C _____
5 rysothi   H _____
6 lobiogy   B _____
7 cmieoocns   E _____

TIME EXPRESSIONS

Time expressions say **when** or **how often** something happens. One type of time expression is *every* + a noun.

I do my homework **every week**. She has an English class **every Wednesday afternoon**. They swim **every morning**.

Another type of time expression is a prepositional phrase for time. The preposition depends on the noun phrase that follows.

- *at* + clock time / weekend: **at** 10 am, **at** 3 pm, **at** the weekend
- *in* + part of the day: **in** the morning, **in** the afternoon, **in** the evening
- *on* + day of the week: **on** Monday, **on** Tuesdays
- *on* + day of the week + part of the day: **on** Monday morning, **on** Tuesday afternoon, **on** Friday evening, **on** Sunday night

6 Write *at*, *in* or *on* in the gaps.

1 Simon swims _____on_____ Saturday morning _____at_____ 8 am.
2 _____ the evening, Abdullah studies in the library.
3 _____ Monday, I have an English class _____ 2 pm.
4 I talk to my family _____ the evening.
5 _____ Tuesday morning, Feride has Maths _____ 11 am.
6 Kyoko goes to the university _____ Monday and Thursday.
7 I do my homework _____ the evening.
8 Andrea goes to work _____ 7 am every day.
9 _____ the weekend, I relax with my friends.

7 Answer the questions. Use the correct time expression.

1 When do you do your homework?

_____

2 What time do you get up?

_____

3 What days do you have classes?

_____

WRITING

CRITICAL THINKING

At the end of this unit, you are going to write about the life of a student in your class. Look at this unit's writing task in the box below.

> ▌ Write about the life of a student in your class.

REMEMBER

1 Work with a partner. Ask and answer the questions about Abdullah.
If you can't remember the answer, look at the text on page 67 for help.

1 What is Abdullah's surname? _____

2 What university does Abdullah go to? _____

3 What courses does he take? _____

4 When does he get up? _____

5 When are his classes? _____

6 When does he meet with his study group? _____

7 When does he go to the library? _____

8 When does he relax with friends? _____

APPLY

2 Now talk with a partner about his or her life. Ask and answer questions like the ones from Exercise 1. Write your partner's answers in the timetable.

What classes do you take? When do you relax with friends?

Name of student: _____   Department: _____

morning

Times	Sun	Mon	Tue	Wed	Thur	Fri	Sat

afternoon

Times	Sun	Mon	Tue	Wed	Thur	Fri	Sat

evening

Times	Sun	Mon	Tue	Wed	Thur	Fri	Sat

3 Now ask your partner to check the timetable and correct any errors.

Choosing relevant information

When you write, make sure that the information you include helps to answer the question. Do not include information which does not help to answer the question.

4 Look at your partner's timetable in Exercise 2. Find three important facts about his or her life. Tell your partner the facts. Does your partner agree or disagree that these are important?

EVALUATE

GRAMMAR FOR WRITING

PARTS OF A SENTENCE

Remember that a simple sentence has a subject and a verb.

subject   *verb*
The Kombai men <u>hunt</u>.

A simple sentence can also have an *object*, a *prepositional phrase* or both. An object is the person or thing that receives the action of a verb.

                                object
The women cook **the food.**

                    prepositional phrase   *prepositional phrase*
Rebecca Moore lived **with the Kombai people** <u>for three months</u>.

              object   *prepositional phrase*
They eat **this food** <u>for breakfast</u>.

1 Work with a partner. Match the sentences (1–4) to the descriptions (a–d).

  1 Abdullah relaxes. _____

  2 He has a busy timetable. _____

  3 Abdullah studies Arab History at university. _____

  4 The Kombai live in the jungle. _____

  a subject + verb + object

  b subject + verb

  c subject + verb + prepositional phrase

  d subject + verb + object + prepositional phrase

2 Match the sentence halves.

1 I do my homework	a have lunch at 1 pm.
2 My friends	b on Saturdays.
3 My sister	c to the gym at 8 am.
4 My brother goes	d eats breakfast at 7 am.

THE PRESENT SIMPLE

Use the *present simple* to talk about daily life.

I have breakfast every morning.

If the subject of the sentence is third person and singular (*he, she, it*), the verb ends with -*s*.

singular		
subject	**verb**	
I You	swim	every day.
He She It	swim**s**	every day.

plural		
subject	**verb**	
We You They	swim	every day.

To make the third person singular form of a verb in the present simple, follow these spelling rules.

rule	third person singular verb form
Add -*s* if the verb ends in a consonant or a consonant sound.	cook ➞ cook**s** live ➞ live**s**
Add -*es* if the verb ends in -*s*, -*z*, -*x*, -*ch* or -*sh*.	pass ➞ pass**es** relax ➞ relax**es** watch ➞ watch**es** wash ➞ wash**es**
Replace -*y* with -*ies* if the verb ends in a consonant + -*y*.	study ➞ stud**ies**
Add -*es* if the verb ends in a vowel sound (*a, e, i, o, u*).	go ➞ go**es**
Add -*s* if the verb ends in a vowel + -*y*.	say ➞ say**s**

Some verbs are irregular. Memorize their spellings. (have ➞ **has**, be ➞ **is**)

GRAMMAR

3 Write the third person singular form of the present simple verb.

infinitive	third person singular verb form
get up	1 gets up
travel	2
go	3
study	4
stay	5
have	6

4 Read the text. Circle the correct forms of the verbs.

Kana (1) *is / are* a student in my class. This (2) *is / are* her timetable. She (3) *study / studies* Management at the University of Brighton. She (4) *get up / gets up* at 6 am. She (5) *eat / eats* breakfast at 6:30 am. On Mondays and Wednesdays, Kana (6) *meet / meets* with a study group at 11 am. She (7) *have / has* lunch at 12:30 pm every day. She (8) *study / studies* in the library from 3 to 6 pm. She (9) *go / goes* to the gym with friends on Sundays. Kana (10) *is / are* a serious student.

5 Write answers to the questions about your partner's timetable on page 72. Use the correct verb form.

1 What does your partner do on Saturdays?

_____

2 What does your partner do every day?

_____

3 When does your partner relax?

_____

4 What does your partner study?

_____

5 When does your partner have classes?

_____

ACADEMIC WRITING SKILLS

MAIN IDEAS AND DETAILS

A *main idea* says what a paragraph is about. The *details* add information about the main idea.

main idea   details

Abdullah Taha is a student in my class. He has a busy timetable.
Abdullah studies Engineering at Cairo University. He takes five courses.
They are Physics, Maths, English, Engineering and Arab History.
His favourite subjects are Physics and Maths.

The main idea is often at the beginning of the paragraph. Then the writer writes details after it. They give more information and explain the main idea.

The main idea in the example is that Abdullah is a student. The details give more information about Abdullah's life as a student. They talk about his school, timetable and courses. Remember that when you write, the details need to be about the main idea.

1 Read the paragraph. Circle the main idea and underline the details. Then choose the correct answer (a–c) to the questions (1 and 2).

> Abdullah has three classes every weekday morning. He gets up at 6 am every day. Then he has Physics from 8 am to 9 am, Maths from 9:15 am to 10:15 am and Engineering from 10:30 am to 11:30 am.

1 What do the details talk about?
  a Abdullah's weekday mornings.
  b Abdullah's English class.
  c Abdullah's weekday afternoons.

2 What detail could the writer also include in this paragraph?
  a Abdullah meets his brother on Sunday afternoons.
  b Abdullah studies in the library in the evening.
  c Abdullah plays football on Wednesday afternoons.

PLUS

2 Read the paragraph. Circle the main idea and underline the details. Then add one more sentence to give another detail. Use your own ideas.

> At the weekends, Abdullah relaxes with friends. Sometimes, he goes to the cinema. _____
> He enjoys his busy life.

WRITING TASK

> Write about the life of a student in your class.

PLAN

1 Look back at the timetable you created for your partner in the Critical thinking section on page 72. Check your notes and add any new information you want to include in your writing. Use it to plan the details for your sentences.

2 Read the Task checklist on page 78 as you prepare your sentences.

WRITE A FIRST DRAFT

3 Write answers in the gaps which are true for your partner.

_____ (*student's name*) is a student in my _____ (*subject*) class. This is _____ (*his / her*) timetable.

4 Write sentences which are true about your partner's schedule.

1 Write a sentence about the subject(s) he / she studies.

_____

2 Write a sentence about the time he / she gets up.

_____

3 Write three sentences about his / her school or university timetable.

_____

_____

_____

4 Write one sentence about his / her weekend or free time.

_____

EDIT

5 Use the Task checklist to review your sentences.

TASK CHECKLIST	✔
Write a sentence which says the main idea.	
Write other sentences which add details.	
Spell present simple third person verbs correctly.	
Use the correct collocations for free-time activities.	
Use the correct prepositions for time expressions.	

6 Make any changes to your sentences.

OBJECTIVES REVIEW

1 Check your learning objectives for this unit. Write *3*, *2* or *1* for each objective.

3 = very well   2 = well   1 = not so well

I can ...

watch and understand a video about visiting Toronto on holiday. _____

annotate a text. _____

choose relevant information. _____

use time expressions. _____

recognize parts of a sentence. _____

use the present simple. _____

write about main ideas and details. _____

write about the life of a student in my class. _____

2 Go to the *Unlock* Online Workbook for more practice with this unit's learning objectives.

WORDLIST		
afternoon (n)	Economics (n) ⊙	meet (v) ⊙
Arabic (n)	English (n) ⊙	morning (n) ⊙
Art (n) ⊙	evening (n) ⊙	Physics (n) ⊙
Biology (n) ⊙	Geography (n)	relax (v)
breakfast (n)	get up (phr v)	Science (n) ⊙
Business (n) ⊙	History (n) ⊙	swim (v)
busy (adj) ⊙	Literature (n)	timetable (n)
Chemistry (n) ⊙	lunch (n)	travel (v) ⊙
cook (v) ⊙	Management (n)	weekdays (n)
dinner (n)	Maths (n)	weekend (n)

⊙ = high-frequency words in the Cambridge Academic Corpus

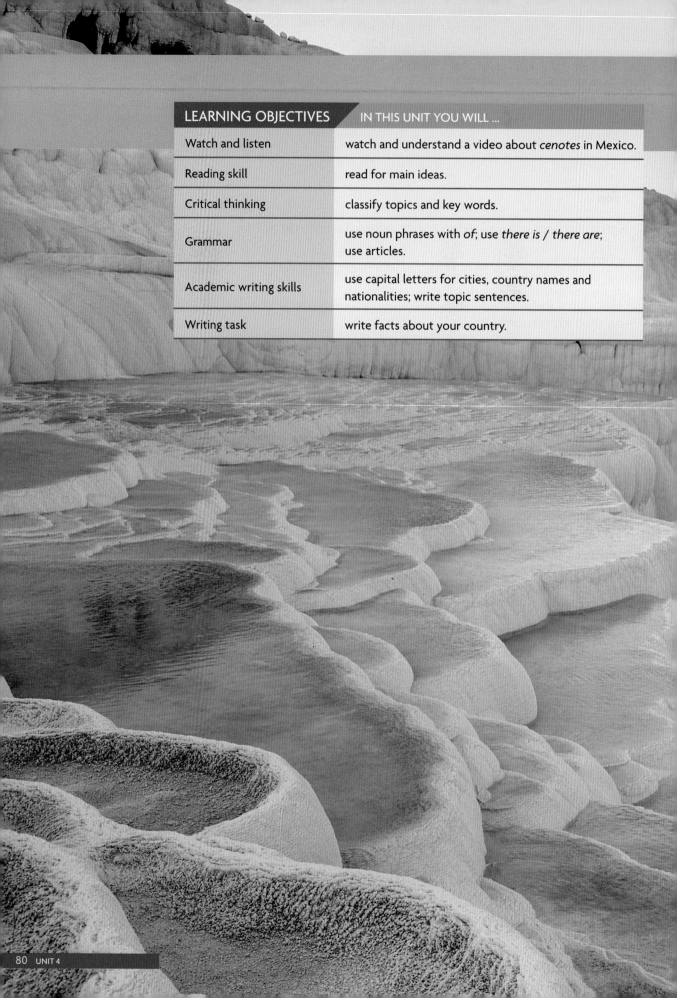

IN THIS UNIT YOU WILL ...

Watch and listen	watch and understand a video about *cenotes* in Mexico.
Reading skill	read for main ideas.
Critical thinking	classify topics and key words.
Grammar	use noun phrases with *of*; use *there is / there are*; use articles.
Academic writing skills	use capital letters for cities, country names and nationalities; write topic sentences.
Writing task	write facts about your country.

PLACES

UNLOCK YOUR KNOWLEDGE

Ask and answer the questions with a partner.

1 What place is in the picture?
2 Why do people go there?
3 Do you want to visit this place? Why / Why not?
4 What places do people visit in your country?

PLUS

   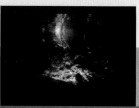

PREPARING TO WATCH

ACTIVATING YOUR KNOWLEDGE

1 Work with a partner and answer the questions.

1 What makes a place special?
2 Why do people like to visit special places?
3 What special place do you want to visit? Why?

PREDICTING CONTENT USING VISUALS

2 Look at the pictures from the video. Put the words in order to make sentences.

1 a monkey / There is / in the forest /.

_____

2 in the trees / a space / There is /.

_____

3 are growing / Plants / in the water /.

_____

4 in the water / is swimming / A man /.

_____

GLOSSARY

space (n) an empty area

full of (adj phr) containing a lot of things

lily pad (n) the large leaf of a water plant that floats on the surface of water, for example, on a lake or pond

turtle (n) an animal with four legs and a hard shell that usually lives in water

WHILE WATCHING

3 ▶ Watch the video. Tick (✔) the true statements.

1 ☐ There aren't many rich, green forests in the Yucatán.
2 ☐ The people in Mexico call the holes in the forests *cenotes*.
3 ☐ These holes are made of wood.
4 ☐ The scientist studies the trees there.
5 ☐ In the Yucatán, *cenotes* are the only places to find fresh water.
6 ☐ Most of the plants and animals live at the top of the *cenotes*.

UNDERSTANDING MAIN IDEAS

4 ▶ Watch again. Write the missing words in the gaps.

1 These amazing holes are the only spaces in the _____ .
2 For Olmo, the *cenotes* are very _____ .
3 _____ is very important in the Yucatán.
4 *Cenotes* help the _____ and plants in the forest live.
5 When Olmo swims far into the cave, it gets _____ and dark.

UNDERSTANDING DETAIL

5 Circle the correct word or phrase.

1 *Cenotes* are *very / not* important in the Yucatán.
2 Animals and plants *need / die in* the *cenotes*.
3 There *is / is no* life in the water.
4 It is *safe / dangerous* to swim far into the cave.

MAKING INFERENCES

DISCUSSION

6 Ask and answer the questions with a partner.

1 Are there any special places in your country like the *cenotes*?
   What are they?
2 Do you want to visit the *cenotes*? Why / Why not?
3 Is it interesting to swim in a cave? Why / Why not?

READING

PREPARING TO READ

UNDERSTANDING KEY VOCABULARY

1 You are going to read a text from a history book. Look at the photos and read the sentences (1–7). Choose the correct definition (a or b) for the words in bold.

1 The Great Lakes in the US are very big, but the **lake** by my house is small.
   a salt water that covers most of the Earth
   b an area of fresh water which has land all around it

2 Lakes have fresh water, but **seas**, like the Mediterranean, have salt water.
   a large areas of very dry land
   b large areas of salt water

3 I do not like to climb **mountains**. I do not like to be up high.
   a very high hills
   b land that is low, near the water

4 There are many trees in a **forest**. They are homes for birds and other animals.
   a a large area of salt water
   b a large area of trees growing closely together

5 The Nile is the longest **river** in the world. It is 6,853 km long.
   a water which flows across the land to a bigger area of water
   b a large area of land with many trees

6 There are five **oceans**. These are the biggest bodies of water in the world.
   a the five main areas of salt water on the Earth
   b an area of sand or rocks next to water

7 People use **maps** to help them find places and understand an area.
   a pictures which show a place and the rivers, lakes and other areas in it
   b boats, cars and other things that people drive

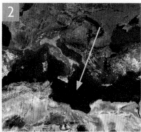

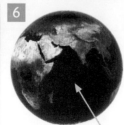

2 Look at the texts and the picture on page 86. Read the questions and choose the correct answers.

page 86

1 What is the book about?
  a the history of the world
  b the history of China
  c the history of maps

2 What does the picture show?
  a a modern map of the world
  b an old map of the world
  c a photograph of the world

WHILE READING

3 Follow the instructions to annotate the text about al-Idrisi's map.

1 Underline the name of an important person in paragraph 1.
2 Underline the name of an important map in paragraph 2.
3 Underline the names of countries that the map shows in paragraph 3.
4 Underline the names of bodies of water the map shows in paragraph 4.

4 Scan the text again and find the continents and countries that are mentioned. Circle them in the table. Then check your answers with a partner.

continents	countries	
Asia	Finland	France
Australia	Spain	Italy
Europe	Norway	England
Africa	Canada	India
North America	Morocco	
South America	China	
Antarctica	The United States	

5 Read Chapter 4.2. Write T (true) or F (false) next to the statements. Correct the false statements.

_____ 1 Muhammad al-Idrisi was Algerian.
_____

_____ 2 The Tabula Rogeriana is written in Greek.
_____

_____ 3 South America is not on the map.
_____

_____ 4 India is on the map.
_____

_____ 5 There are lakes on the map.
_____

Take a look!

A world history of maps
by J. T. Kirk

Add to Basket

★★★★★

Price: from £16.75

Book sections

▶ Table of contents

Introduction

Chapter 4.2

Table of contents

A world history of maps
by J. T. Kirk

Add to Basket

★★★★★

Price: from £16.75

Book sections

Introduction

▶ Chapter 4.2

4.2

Figure 4.3: World map by Muhammad al-Idrisi, 1154

1 Muhammad al-Idrisi came from Morocco. He studied in North Africa and Spain. As a young man, he travelled in Spain, North Africa, France, England and parts of Asia. In 1154, he began working for King Roger II of Sicily. Al-Idrisi created his **map** of the world then.

2 Al-Idrisi's map of the world is called the Tabula Rogeriana in Europe. The map is in Arabic. Al-Idrisi used information from earlier Arab and Greek maps. He also used information from explorers. These men were sent to the different countries to draw and record what they saw. This map helped people travel from country to country.

3 The map shows North Africa, Europe and South and East Asia. There are many European countries on the map. There is Norway in the north, Spain in the west and Italy in the south. The map also shows India and China.

4 There are **forests, rivers, lakes, mountains, seas** and **oceans** on the map. Al-Idrisi's map shows the Mediterranean Sea, the Indian Ocean and the river Nile.

DISCUSSION

6 Ask and answer the questions with a partner.

1 How did al-Idrisi make his map?
2 What can you learn from a very old map?
3 When do you use maps?

READING 2

PREPARING TO READ

1 Ask and answer the questions with a partner.

1 What are important businesses in your country?
2 How many people live in your country?
3 What is the climate in your country?
4 What languages do people speak in your country?

USING YOUR
KNOWLEDGE

2 You are going to read a fact file about an island country. Read the sentences (1–8). Write the words in bold next to the correct definitions (a–h).

UNDERSTANDING
KEY VOCABULARY

1 Mauritius is an **island** in the Indian Ocean.
2 Riyadh is the **capital** of Saudi Arabia.
3 Many people enjoy the water and sun at the **beach**.
4 **Modern** cities have new buildings, parks and businesses.
5 Arizona is **famous** because it has the Grand Canyon. Many people visit there.
6 I visited Rome as a **tourist** because it is a beautiful place.
7 My school is **international**. There are students from all over the world.
8 Coffee with milk is **popular** in my country. Everyone drinks it. It's really good.

a _____ (n) a person who travels and visits places for fun
b _____ (adj) made with new ideas and designs
c _____ (n) land with water all around it
d _____ (n) an area of sand or rocks next to a sea, ocean or lake
e _____ (n) the most important city in a country, where the government is
f _____ (adj) many people know it
g _____ (adj) many people like it
h _____ (adj) relating to or involving two or more countries

The Maldives
AN OVERVIEW

1 The Maldives are **islands** in the Indian Ocean. The islands are near Sri Lanka. The Maldives are **famous** for their good climate, beautiful **beaches** and warm seas.

2 There are 440,000 people in the Maldives. Most people live on small islands.

3 The **capital** of the Maldives is Malé. It is a **modern** city with an **international** airport and a big harbour[1].

4 People in Malé speak English and Dhivehi. English is useful because many **tourists** come here.

5 Tourism and fishing are very important businesses in the Maldives. There are many tourist hotels. Many people work there. Others work as fishermen or in fish factories[2]. The currency is the rufiyaa.

[1]**harbour** (n) area of water next to land for ships and boats
[2]**factories** (n) buildings where a large number of things or products are made
[3]**currency** (n) the money a country uses
[4]**industry** (n) types of businesses

FACT FILE
FULL NAME: Republic of Maldives
POPULATION: 440,000
CAPITAL: Malé
GEOGRAPHY: 1,190 islands
CLIMATE: good, average temperature +30 °C
LANGUAGES: Dhivehi and English
RELIGION: Islam
CURRENCY[3]: rufiyaa
INDUSTRY[4]: tourism and fishing

INDIA

Maldives

Sri Lanka

•Malé

one of the Maldives' beautiful beaches

MEET THE LOCALS
Ahmed Faiz, 19

6 I live on an island south of Malé. Life on my island is very simple. There are some shops and there is one mosque. We speak Dhivehi but we also learn English in high school. It is a nice place to live.

7 The Maldives are famous for their fish. There is a **popular** fish soup here. It is called *garudiya*. It is delicious.

8 People in the Maldives like to swim and dive.

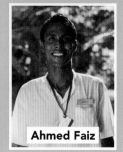

Ahmed Faiz

Reading for main ideas

Many texts have paragraphs. A paragraph is part of a long text. Each paragraph has one topic or main idea. When we read for the main ideas in a text, we read each paragraph to find:
- the topic (e.g. family, weather, university)
- the important information about the topic (e.g. the number of brothers and sisters a person has; the average rainfall in summer; the reason a student wants to study)

Tourism and fishing are very important businesses in the Maldives. There are many tourist hotels. Many people work there. Others work as fishermen or in fish factories. The currency is the rufiyaa.

The topic here is tourism and fishing. The important information about the topic is that they are very important businesses in the Maldives.

3 Read the text on page 88. Write the topics from the box next to the paragraph numbers in the table. Then write the important information about the topics.

READING FOR
MAIN IDEAS

> languages   the population   hobbies and sport   the capital city
> where the Maldives are   a young Maldivian's home
> traditional food   ~~tourism and fishing~~

paragraph	topic	important information about the topic
1		
2		
3		
4		
5	tourism and fishing	they are very important businesses in the Maldives
6		
7		
8		

DISCUSSION

4 Work with a partner. Use ideas from Reading 1 and Reading 2. Ask and answer the questions.

1 Why do tourists go to the Maldives?
2 Do you want to visit the Maldives? Why / Why not?
3 Why do people travel to different countries? What's important to know about a country?

⊙ LANGUAGE DEVELOPMENT

NOUN PHRASES WITH *OF*

One type of noun phrase is a noun + *of* + a noun.

    noun   *noun*   *noun*   *noun*

Bogota is **the capital of Colombia**. Madrid is in **the centre of Spain**.

The noun phrase noun + *of* + noun answers the question *What?*

This book is about **history**. (The history of what?)
This book is about **the history of Japan**.

1 Match the sentence halves.

1 The capital
2 The dollar is the currency
3 The main languages
4 Al-Idrisi's map shows parts

a of the United States.
b of Asia.
c of Canada are English and French.
d of the Maldives is Malé.

2 Work with a partner. Use a noun + *of* + noun to answer the questions.

1 What country is Lisbon the capital of?

_____

2 What is the capital of your country?

_____

3 What is the currency of your country?

_____

4 What are the main languages of your country?

_____

VOCABULARY FOR PLACES

3 Write the words from the box in the correct places (1–10) on the picture.

> beach   cliff   desert   farm   field   forest
> hill   mountain   sea   valley

PLUS

1. _____

2. _____

3. _____

4. _____

5. _____

6. _____

7. _____

8. _____

9. _____

10. _____

WRITING

CRITICAL THINKING

At the end of this unit, you are going to write about your country. Look at this unit's writing task in the box below.

Write facts about your country.

SKILLS

Classifying topics and key words

Classifying means putting words into groups with the same topic. Classifying helps you to plan your writing.

A writer thinks about words to describe his or her country.

tourism   language   fishing   Dhivehi   industry   English

Then the writer classifies the words to organize and plan.

topic	key words
industry	tourism fishing
language	English Dhivehi

 UNDERSTAND

1 Look at Reading 2 on page 88. Circle the key words which the writer used to discuss each topic.

topic	key words
geography	islands climate food Indian Ocean near Sri Lanka
language	English Thai Dhivehi
industry	tourism fishing cooking currency diving

 APPLY

2 Find the paragraphs in Reading 2 with the topics in the table below. Then list the key words.

topic	key words
capital	
population	

3 Think about your country. Choose five topics from the box and write these in column A.

> capital   climate   currency   food   geography
> industry   language   population   sport

A topic	B key words

4 Think of key words for the topics and write them in column B.

5 Without showing your table, tell a partner your key words. Can your partner guess your topic? If your partner is wrong, you may need to choose different key words.

ANALYZE

GRAMMAR FOR WRITING

THERE IS / THERE ARE

GRAMMAR

You can use *there is / there are* to say that something exists. Use *there is* before singular nouns and *there are* before plural nouns.

singular:

There is an airport in Malé.
There is a mosque on Ahmed Faiz's island.
There is a popular fish soup in the Maldives.

plural:

There are many countries on al-Idrisi's map.
There are many tourist resorts in the Maldives.
There are 440,000 people in the Maldives.

PLUS

1 Read the sentences. Write *There is / There are* in the gaps.

1 _____ many different kinds of businesses in my country.
2 _____ 50 states in the USA.
3 _____ three airports in my city.
4 _____ a big art museum in Seoul.
5 _____ a beautiful park in my city.

2 Read the sentences. Tick (✔) the correct sentences and put a cross (✘) next to the incorrect sentences.

_____ 1 There are many different people in London.
_____ 2 There is mountains in Switzerland.
_____ 3 There is many parks in Tokyo.
_____ 4 In Thailand, there are many islands.
_____ 5 There have many people in Buenos Aires.
_____ 6 There are many tourists in Paris.
_____ 7 They are many lakes in Italy.
_____ 8 There are a big river in my city.

3 Correct the incorrect sentences in Exercise 2.

_____

_____

_____

_____

_____

ARTICLES

Use *articles* before a noun or before an adjective + noun.

Indefinite articles (*a / an*)

A / An is the indefinite article. Use *a / an* with singular countable nouns.

Use *a* before consonant sounds.
- **a** river, **a** lake, **a** sea, **a** mountain
- **a** big river, **a** small lake, **a** cold sea, **a** tall mountain

Use *an* before vowel sounds.
- **an** ocean, **an** island, **an** hour
- **an** old city, **an** ancient map

Definite article (*the*)

The is the definite article. Use *the* before the names of singular or plural places:
- rivers – **the** river Danube, **the** river Nile, **the** river Thames
- seas – **the** North Sea, **the** Mediterranean Sea, **the** Black Sea
- oceans – **the** Pacific Ocean, **the** Atlantic Ocean, **the** Indian Ocean
- many famous places – **the** Galata Tower, **the** Eiffel Tower, **the** Pyramids
- 'united' countries – **the** United Arab Emirates, **the** United Kingdom, **the** United States of America
- groups of islands – **the** Maldives, **the** Azores
- groups of mountains – **the** Andes, **the** Alps, **the** Himalayas
- plural countries – **the** Philippines, **the** Maldives

Zero article

Use no article (the *zero article*) before the names of:
- continents – Asia, North America, Europe
- most countries – England, China, Turkey
- cities – Abu Dhabi, Bangkok, Shanghai
- lakes – Lake Superior, Lake Baikal

4 Read the sentences and write *a, an, the* or Ø (*zero article*) in the gaps.

1 My grandparents' house is next to _____ lake.
2 My parents live on _____ island in _____ Mediterranean Sea.
3 My family comes from _____ Chile.
4 _____ Chile is in _____ South America.
5 We live near _____ Pacific Ocean.
6 _____ Andes are the highest mountains in my country.
7 My sister lives in _____ United Kingdom.
8 She works in _____ Tokyo. She lives in _____ small village.

5 Correct the mistakes in the sentences.

1 I come from the India.

_____

2 Paris is an popular city with tourists.

_____

3 There is very tall building in Abu Dhabi.

_____

4 I go to an university in Dublin.

_____

5 United Kingdom is in a Europe.

_____

6 I live by big lake.

_____

7 Ural Mountains are in Russia.

_____

8 He studies in a United Kingdom.

_____

9 The Turkey is a beautiful country.

_____

10 There is big mountain near my city.

_____

6 Work with a partner. Answer the questions. Use the correct articles.

1 What sea or ocean is close to the country you live in?

_____

2 What place do tourists visit in the country you live in?

_____

3 What island do you want to visit?

_____

4 What countries are close to the country you live in?

_____

ACADEMIC WRITING SKILLS

SPELLING AND PUNCTUATION

Capital letters

The first letter of the name of a city, the name of a country and the adjective for a nationality is always a *capital letter*.

1 Look at the country names and write vowels (*a, e, i, o, u*) in the gaps to make the correct nationality names.

country	nationality
China	Ch ____ n ____ s ____
India	____ nd ____ ____ n
Egypt	____ gypt ____ ____ n
Saudi Arabia	S ____ ____ d ____
The United Arab Emirates	____ m ____ r ____ t ____
Algeria	____ lg ____ r ____ ____ n
Japan	J ____ p ____ n ____ s ____
Thailand	Th ____ ____
Turkey	T ____ rk ____ sh
France	Fr ____ nch
The United Kingdom	Br ____ t ____ sh
Canada	C ____ n ____ d ____ ____ n

2 Correct the punctuation in the sentences. Add capital letters and full stops.

1 i am from cairo

_____

2 there are many beautiful beaches in portugal

_____

3 the climate is good in the maldives

_____

4 there are four main islands in japan

_____

5 chicken is very popular in malaysia

_____

Paragraphs are groups of sentences which talk about one idea. This is called the *main idea*. Good paragraphs have three parts: a *topic sentence, supporting sentences / details* and a *concluding sentence*.

The topic sentence usually comes first. The details, also called the supporting sentences, come next and give more information about the main idea. The paragraph ends with a concluding sentence.

topic sentence	I live on an island south of Malé.		
supporting sentences / details	Life on my island is very simple.	There are some shops and there is one mosque.	We speak Dhivehi, but we also learn English in high school.
concluding sentence	It is a nice place to live.		

Topic sentences

The topic sentence tells the reader what the paragraph is about. It tells the main idea of the paragraph. In the paragraph above, the topic is 'an island south of Malé'. The main idea in the topic sentence is that it is where the writer lives. The topic sentence is usually the first sentence in a paragraph. Then the following sentences add details to the topic.

3 Read each group of sentences. Underline the topic sentence in each.

1 The Maldives are islands in the Indian Ocean. The islands are near Sri Lanka. The Maldives are famous for their good climate, beautiful beaches and warm seas.

2 Tourism and fishing are very important businesses in the Maldives. There are many tourist hotels. Many people work there. Others work as fishermen or in fish factories. The currency is the rufiyaa.

4 Read each group of sentences (1–2). Choose the correct topic sentence (a–c). Then compare with a partner.

1 The mountains are beautiful, but people also enjoy the forests and lakes in Canada. It's a popular tourist place.
   a Toronto is a big city in Canada.
   b Many people come to visit Canada every year.
   c Canada is a large country.

2 There are many restaurants and there is a public market. You can buy fresh fish, vegetables and other delicious food there. Everyone loves eating in Rome.
   a Eating is an important part of visiting Rome.
   b You can do many things in Rome.
   c Rome is the capital of Italy.

Rome, Italy

5 Read the sentences below and write your own topic sentence. Then compare with a partner.

Many people live in the capital. There are lots of things to do and see. It is a busy and interesting place to live.

_____ .

WRITING TASK

▶ Write facts about your country.

PLAN

1 Look back at the notes you created about your country in the Critical thinking section on page 93. Choose three topics to write paragraphs about. Check the key words and phrases you will use and add any new information you want to include in your writing.

2 Read the Task checklist on page 100 as you prepare your paragraphs.

WRITE A FIRST DRAFT

3 Write a paragraph for each topic. Write a topic sentence and one or two supporting sentences for each topic. Use the key words to help you.

The capital of my country is Bangkok. It is a famous city in Thailand. There are more than eight million people living there.

EDIT

4 Use the Task checklist to review your paragraphs.

TASK CHECKLIST	✔
Write three short paragraphs.	
Write a topic sentence for each paragraph.	
Write one or two supporting sentences for each topic sentence.	
Use *there is* before singular nouns and *there are* before plural nouns.	
Use *the* before the names of rivers, seas, oceans, some countries and famous places.	
Use the zero article before the names of continents, some countries and cities.	

5 Make any necessary changes to your paragraphs.

OBJECTIVES REVIEW

1 Check your learning objectives for this unit. Write *3, 2* or *1* for each objective.

3 = very well   2 = well   1 = not so well

I can ...

watch and understand a video about *cenotes* in Mexico. ⎯⎯⎯

read for main ideas. ⎯⎯⎯

classify topics and key words. ⎯⎯⎯

use noun phrases with *of*. ⎯⎯⎯

use *there is / there are*. ⎯⎯⎯

use articles. ⎯⎯⎯

use capital letters for cities, country names and nationalities. ⎯⎯⎯

write topic sentences. ⎯⎯⎯

write facts about my country. ⎯⎯⎯

2 Go to the *Unlock* Online Workbook for more practice with this unit's learning objectives.

WORDLIST

beach (n)	hill (n) ⊙	popular (adj) ⊙
capital (n) ⊙	international (adj) ⊙	river (n) ⊙
cliff (n)	island (n) ⊙	sea (n) ⊙
desert (n) ⊙	lake (n) ⊙	tourist (n)
famous (adj) ⊙	map (n) ⊙	valley (n) ⊙
farm (n) ⊙	modern (adj) ⊙	
field (n) ⊙	mountain (n) ⊙	
forest (n) ⊙	ocean (n) ⊙	

⊙ = high-frequency words in the Cambridge Academic Corpus

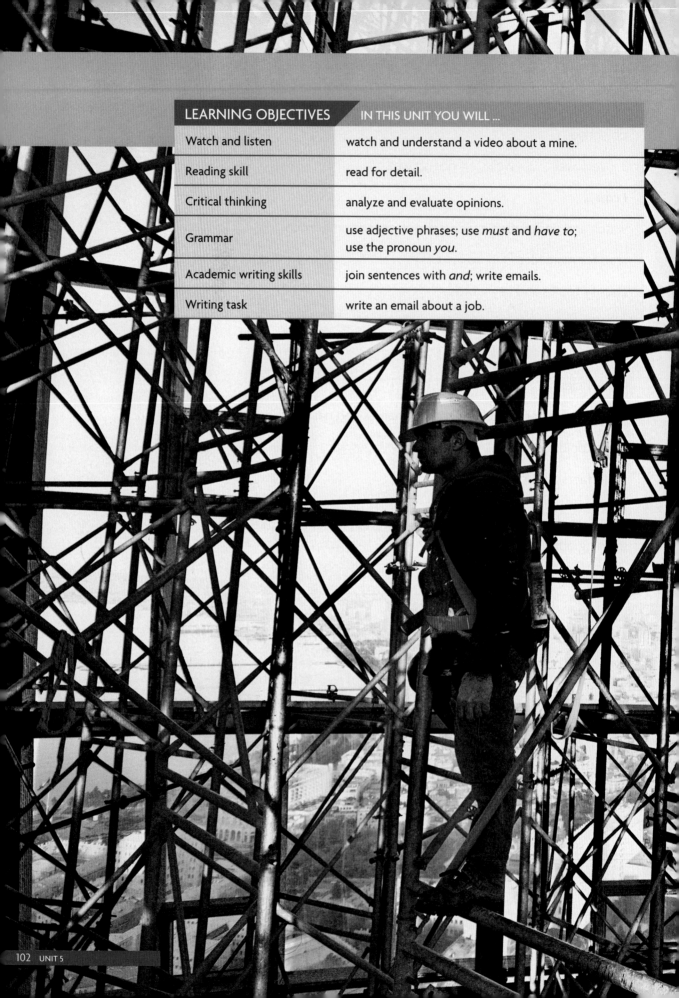

LEARNING OBJECTIVES

IN THIS UNIT YOU WILL ...

Watch and listen	watch and understand a video about a mine.
Reading skill	read for detail.
Critical thinking	analyze and evaluate opinions.
Grammar	use adjective phrases; use *must* and *have to*; use the pronoun *you*.
Academic writing skills	join sentences with *and*; write emails.
Writing task	write an email about a job.

UNLOCK YOUR KNOWLEDGE

Look at the photo. Ask and answer the questions with a partner.

1 What are the men doing? What is their job?
2 Do you want this job? Why / Why not?
3 What makes a job good?
4 What job do you want? What job do you not want?

PLUS

WATCH AND LISTEN

PREPARING TO WATCH

ACTIVATING YOUR
KNOWLEDGE

1 Work with a partner and answer the questions.

   1 Do you work? What do you do?
   2 What are some unusual jobs?
   3 What are some dangerous jobs?
   4 Would you like to have an unusual job? Why / Why not?

PREDICTING
CONTENT USING
VISUALS

2 Look at the pictures from the video. Match the sentence halves.

   1 There is a large   a much bigger than the man.
   2 The truck is carrying b are flying in the air.
   3 The truck is   c hole in the ground.
   4 The earth and rocks   d a lot of rocks and earth.

GLOSSARY

---

copper (n) a soft, red-brown metal

mine (n) a hole in the ground where people get gold, salt, etc.

produce (v) to make or grow something

wire (n) a long, very thin piece of metal

dig (v) to make a hole in the ground

giant (adj) very big

WHILE WATCHING

3 ▶ Watch the video. Write *T* (true) or *F* (false) next to the statements. Correct the false statements.

UNDERSTANDING MAIN IDEAS

_____ 1 The Bingham mine is in Utah.

_____

_____ 2 The mine produces enough copper wires for all the homes in Canada.

_____

_____ 3 We use copper wires in a lot of different places.

_____

_____ 4 The trucks work 12 hours a day.

_____

4 ▶ Watch again. Circle the words you hear.

UNDERSTANDING DETAIL

1 It is the *largest* / *longest* mine of its kind in the world.
2 It is almost *one mile* / *two and a half miles* deep.
3 The rocks contain a *large* / *small* amount of copper.
4 They also use something *stronger* / *weaker* to get the rocks and copper out of the ground.

5 Tick (✔) the true sentences about work in the Bingham mine.

MAKING INFERENCES

1 ☐ It is difficult.
2 ☐ It can be dangerous.
3 ☐ The truck drivers work in the office for half of the day.
4 ☐ The operations manager has an important job.
5 ☐ Finding copper can take a long time.
6 ☐ There are many mines in Utah.

DISCUSSION

6 Ask and answer the questions with a partner.

1 Is working in the Bingham mine an interesting job? Why / Why not?
2 Are there any mines in your country or region? What do they produce?
3 Do you know any other dangerous jobs? What are they?

READING

PREPARING TO READ

USING YOUR
KNOWLEDGE

1 Ask and answer the questions with a partner.

1 What makes someone good at his or her job?
2 What information do you want to know before you take a job?
3 Where are good places to find information about different types of jobs?

PREVIEWING

2 Look at the texts on page 108. Where are they from?

a a website about travel
b a website for jobs
c a website for teachers

UNDERSTANDING
KEY VOCABULARY

3 You are going to read online job adverts. Read the sentences (1–8). Choose the correct definitions (a or b) for the words in bold.

1 I am **fit**. I run 5 kilometres every day.
   a in good health; strong
   b have a lot of money

2 My mum is a doctor. She works at a **hospital**.
   a a place where people who are sick or hurt go for help
   b a place where people go to study and learn

3 Miriam needs two teaspoons of **medicine**. She is not feeling well.
   a a sandwich or a salad
   b something you take to feel better

4 Oscar is a **pilot**. He can fly planes and passed a flying test.
   a a person who teaches children
   b a person who flies an aeroplane

5 Football players get good **pay**. They make millions of pounds a year.
   a the money you receive for doing a job
   b the feeling you get from doing good work

6 I have **friendly** teachers. They always say 'hi' and smile when I see them.
   a nice and kind
   b not nice or kind

7 The **nurse** checked the boy's temperature. He was not feeling well.
   a a person who helps doctors and cares for people
   b a person who helps children learn at school

8 I am **healthy**. I eat food which is good for me. I sleep well. I go to the gym.
   a quick to understand; intelligent
   b being well; not sick

WHILE READING

4 Scan the texts on page 108. Write words from the texts in the gaps (1–8).

	text A	text B	text C
1 What is the job?	(1)	pilot	(2)
2 Which country is the job in?	(3)	(4)	Japan
3 Where is the work?	Renji Hospital	(5)	Kitahiroshima Primary School
4 What is the pay?	CNY 16,800 per month	(6)	(7)
5 What are the hours?	full time (including weekends)	part time	(8)

Reading for detail

Reading for detail means looking for key words which give more information about the main idea. One way of reading for detail is to follow the steps below:

- Ask a question: *What is the job at Renji Hospital?*
- Scan the text to find key words: *looking for, hospital, teach, nurses*
- Read the sentences in the paragraph with the key words to find the correct answer: *are looking for a nurse to work at the hospital and teach student nurses*

5 Read the texts again. Write *T* (true) or *F* (false) next to the statements. Correct the false statements.

_____ 1 The pilot at FlyHigh must speak three languages.

_____ 2 The teacher at Kitahiroshima Primary School has to teach grades 1–2.

_____ 3 The nurse at Renji Hospital must have ten years' experience.

_____ 4 Teachers at Kitahiroshima Primary School are friendly.

_____ 5 Pilots at FlyHigh are paid per hour.

_____ 6 The nurse at Renji Hospital must speak two languages.

FIND_MY_JOB.COM

[FIND A JOB]   [GET HELP!]   [UPLOAD YOUR CV]

A

🔍 YOUR SEARCH ✕

Area(s): Medicine

Job(s): Nurse

✉ Email me jobs like this

📶 RSS Feeds

Location[1]: Shanghai, China

Renji **Hospital**

Renji Hospital is in Shanghai. We train and teach doctors and **nurses**.

We are looking for a nurse to work at the hospital and teach student nurses. You have to work early mornings and late nights. You must also give **medicine** to patients.

You must have ten years' experience[2]. You must also speak Chinese and English.

Pay: CNY 16,800 per month

Hours: Full time (including weekends)

B

🔍 YOUR SEARCH ✕

Area(s): Aviation

Job(s): Pilot

✉ Email me jobs like this

📶 RSS Feeds

Location: Mumbai, India

FlyHigh Air Transport Company

FlyHigh is a small company in Mumbai, India. We have private[3] flights throughout Asia.

We are looking for a **pilot**. All our pilots are **friendly** and speak English, Hindi and Urdu.

You must have two years' experience. You have to work weekends. You must be **fit** and **healthy**.

Pay: INR 200,000 per journey

Hours: Part time

C

🔍 YOUR SEARCH ✕

Area(s): Education

Job(s): Teacher

✉ Email me jobs like this

📶 RSS Feeds

Location: Kitahiroshima, Japan

Kitahiroshima Primary School

Kitahiroshima is a private English school. Our teachers are friendly and interested in teaching children.

We are looking for a Maths teacher to teach grades 1–3.

You must have a university education. You must speak English.

Pay: JPY 320,000 per month

Hours: Full time

---

[1]**location** (n) a place
[2]**experience** (n) what you know from doing your job
[3]**private** (adj) belongs to one person or group

DISCUSSION

6 Ask and answer the questions with a partner.

1 For which job do you need to speak more than one language? Why do you think they ask for that?
2 Which job from Reading 1 do you want to do? Why?

READING 2

PREPARING TO READ

1 Think about the emails you write to your friends.

1 Why do you write them?
2 What do you write about?
3 Is your language the same when you write as when you speak?

2 Work with a partner on page 108. Compare your answers in Exercise 1. What is the same? What is different?

PLUS

USING YOUR
KNOWLEDGE

UNDERSTANDING
KEY VOCABULARY

3 You are going to read emails about job searches. Read the sentences (1–7). Write the words and phrases in bold next to the correct definitions (a–g).

1 Science is very **interesting**. There is so much to learn and know.
2 I work for a **company** which makes computers.
3 Yusuf works at a **gym**. He teaches people to do exercises.
4 My sister is very **good at** cricket. She is the best player on the team.
5 I need to do well in **high school** so I can go to a good university.
6 My mum is an **engineer**. She plans and builds parts for cars.
7 School is **great**. I really like it and I'm learning a lot. It's going well.

a _____ (n) a person who designs and builds things
b _____ (n) an organization which sells something to make money
c _____ (n) a school for children from about 12 to 18 years old
d _____ (adj) able to do something well
e _____ (n) a place with machines where people go to do exercises
f _____ (adj) very good; excellent
g _____ (adj) exciting; not boring

PLUS

A

To: a_evgin@cup.org
From: k_t_h1001@cup.org
Subject: **Interesting** job for you!

Hi, Ahmad!

I've found a **great** job for you. It's for a full-time fitness instructor[1]. The job is at David Allen's Irish **Gym** in Manchester.

You have to get up early in the morning. There are 12 students in each group. You have to be very friendly and **good at** sports. The pay is very good – they pay £28 an hour. You don't have to work on Fridays.

I think you'll like this job. Here's the link[2]: www.ukjobs.co.uk/Fitness-instructor

Talk to you soon!

Karel

B

To: erik1221@cup.org
From: ingrid_soljberg@cup.org
Subject: IT'S MUM – LOOK AT THIS JOB!

Erik,

I've found a great job for you. It's in Oslo and I know you want to live there. Here's the link: www.itcompany42.org/jobs I know this **company**.

The job is for a software[3] **engineer**. They pay £4,150 per month!

You must have studied Computer Science at university, and you have to have two years' experience. It also says that you must know some Norwegian. You don't have to speak Norwegian a lot, so it's OK for you.

Let me know what you think!

Love,

Mum

C

To: daria_122@cup.org
From: olly_murgatroyd@cup.org
Subject: Do you want a job in a great country?

Dear Daria,

I hope you're well. I have a great job for you. I think you'll like it. It's in South Korea! I know you love Korean food.

The job is in Suncheon. It's a small city in the south of the country.

The job is at a **high school**. You have to teach English and French to grades 10 to 12. You speak English and French (and Russian!).

You don't have to speak Korean, so this is a great job for you. You have to work many hours every day. But you are a very serious teacher. I know you work hard.

Here's the link: www.skoreajobs.com/Education/HS/Languages

Good luck!

Oliver

---

[1]**instructor** (n) somebody who teaches
[2]**link** (n) a word or phrase on a website which takes you to another website
[3]**software** (n) programs which you use to make a computer do different things

WHILE READING

4 Scan the texts on page 110. Write the correct information in the gaps.

1 The email to Ahmad is about a job as a _____ .
2 There are _____ students in a class at the gym.
3 The email to Erik is about a job as a _____ .
4 The pay for Erik's job is _____ per month.
5 The job for Daria is in _____ .
6 Daria must teach grades _____ to _____ .

SCANNING TO FIND INFORMATION

5 Read the texts again. Choose the answer that best states the main ideas.

a Each email is from a company. The company gives information about a job.
b Each email is about a teaching job. The emails talk about the languages the person needs to speak.
c Each email is from a family member or friend. The person talks about a job.
d Each email is from a person looking for a job. The person says why the job is great.

READING FOR MAIN IDEAS

6 Read the texts again. Write *A* (Ahmad), *E* (Erik) or *D* (Daria) next to the statements.

1 He / She must be good at sport. _____
2 He / She has to teach two languages. _____
3 He / She must have two years' experience. _____
4 He / She has to get up early. _____
5 He / She must work many hours every day. _____

READING FOR DETAIL

DISCUSSION

7 Ask and answer the questions with a partner.

1 Which jobs from Reading 2 are you interested in? Why?
2 Do you want to move to a different country for a job? Why / Why not?
3 What information did the job adverts in Reading 1 and emails in Reading 2 include about the jobs? What other information is important to know when you look for a job?

SYNTHESIZING

VOCABULARY FOR JOBS

1 Make sentences about jobs. Write the verb phrases from the box in the correct places in column B of the table.

> grows food and looks after animals   writes news stories   plays a sport in a team
> teaches children   ~~gives people medicine~~   manages people
> teaches people to do exercises   cares for sick people
> makes software for computers   teaches languages

A jobs	B activities	C locations
1 A farmer		on a farm.
2 A manager		
3 A doctor	gives people medicine	
4 A journalist		in an office.
5 A software engineer		
6 A football player		in big cities.
7 A school teacher		
8 A fitness instructor		
9 A nurse		
10 A language teacher		

PLUS

2 Write the prepositional phrases from the box in the correct places in column C of the table. You can use some phrases more than once. Remember to write the full stop.

> in a hospital.   in an office.   in a school.
> in a gym.   in a company.

ADJECTIVE PHRASES

An *adjective phrase* describes the subject of the sentence. The adjective phrase comes after the verb *be*.

One type of adjective phrase is *very* + adjective.

Software engineers are **very intelligent**. Nurses must be **very kind**.

Another type of adjective phrase is adjective + *and* + adjective.

Fitness instructors are **fit and healthy**. Nurses have to be **kind and helpful**.

Adjectives with prepositional phrases

Another type of adjective phrase is *good at* + noun or *good with* + noun.

The teacher is **good at Maths**. Nurses must be **good with people**.

Usually people are *good at* a subject and *good with* a person or object.

3 Read the sentences and circle the best words and phrases.

1 Fitness instructors have to be *interesting / healthy and strong*. They are moving around all day!
2 Doctors must be *very intelligent / very healthy and strong*. There is a lot to know about medicine.
3 Nurses have to be *friendly / strong*. They work with people.
4 Farmers have to be *strong / friendly*. They work with animals and equipment.

PLUS

4 Circle the correct preposition in each sentence.

1 A primary school teacher has to be good *at / with* children.
2 A software engineer needs to be good *at / with* computers.
3 A nurse needs to be good *at / with* people.
4 A French and Spanish teacher needs to be good *at / with* languages.
5 A journalist needs to be good *at / with* writing.

WRITING

CRITICAL THINKING

At the end of this unit, you are going to write an email. Look at this unit's writing task in the box below.

▎ Write an email about a job.

SKILLS

Analyzing and evaluating opinions

It is useful to know what people think about a topic. This is their opinion. Then you can use the information to make decisions. One way to get people's opinions is with a *Likert scale*. In a Likert scale, people read a sentence and then circle the answer that is true for them. Their answer shows how they feel.

I am good at English.

1   2   3   ④   5

1 = strongly disagree   **4** = agree
2 = disagree   **5** = strongly agree
3 = neither agree nor disagree

EVALUATE

1 Read the sentences and circle the answers which are true for you.

1 = strongly disagree	4 = agree
2 = disagree	5 = strongly agree
3 = neither agree nor disagree	

1 I am healthy.
   1   2   3   4   5

2 I am fit and strong.
   1   2   3   4   5

3 I am good with people.
   1   2   3   4   5

4 I am very intelligent.
   1   2   3   4   5

5 I am kind and helpful.
   1   2   3   4   5

6 I am good with children.
   1   2   3   4   5

7 I am very good at football.
   1   2   3   4   5

8 I am good at Maths.
   1   2   3   4   5

9 I am good at writing.
   1   2   3   4   5

10 I am good with computers.
   1   2   3   4   5

11 I am good with animals.
   1   2   3   4   5

12 I am good at languages.
   1   2   3   4   5

2 Work with a partner. Underline the adjective phrases in the sentences in Exercise 1.

3 Look at the jobs (1–10) in the table. For each job, write the adjective phrase(s) from Exercise 1 which describe(s) it. The first one has been done for you.

ANALYZE

A job	B best description
1 a farmer	*good with animals*
2 a manager	
3 a doctor	
4 a journalist	
5 a software engineer	
6 a football player	
7 a school teacher	
8 a fitness instructor	
9 a nurse	
10 a language teacher	

4 Work with a partner. Read your partner's answers to Exercise 1. Then look at the table in Exercise 3 and choose the best job for your partner. Does your partner agree?

EVALUATE

GRAMMAR FOR WRITING

MUST AND HAVE TO

Use *must* + infinitive or *have to* + infinitive to say that something is necessary.
Doctors **must be** intelligent. Doctors **have to be** intelligent.

Use *must* + infinitive for *I, you, he, she, it, we* and *they*.
They **must be** kind.

Never use *must to* + infinitive.
~~A nurse must to be kind and helpful.~~ → A nurse **must be** kind and helpful.

Use *have to* + infinitive for *I, you, we* and *they*.
Managers **have to be** good with people. They **have to be** good with people.

Use *has to* + infinitive for *he, she* and *it*.
A manager **has to be** good with people. He / She **has to be** good with people.

1 Correct the mistakes in the sentences.

1 A football player musts be strong and healthy.
2 Pilots have work at night.
3 A manager have to be helpful.
4 Teachers must good with people.
5 A software engineer must to be good at Maths.
6 Farmers have good with animals.
7 Journalists must to good at writing.
8 A language teacher must good at speaking and writing.

Do not have to / Does not have to

Use *do not have to / does not have to* + infinitive to say that something is not necessary. You can use contractions for *do not* (*don't*) and *does not* (*doesn't*).

Use *do not have to* + infinitive for *I, you, we* and *they*.
Farmers **do not (don't) have to** be good with computers.

Use *does not have to* + infinitive for *he, she* and *it*.
A language teacher **does not (doesn't) have to** be good at Maths.

Do <u>not</u> use *must not* + infinitive to say that something is not necessary.
~~A journalist must not be good with animals.~~ → A journalist **does not (doesn't) have to** be good with animals.

2 Put the words in order to make sentences.

1 does / have to / A farmer / with people / not / be good / .

_____

2 A software engineer / does not / be / patient and / kind / have to / .

_____

3 with animals / have / not / do / Nurses / to be good / .

_____

4 be strong / You / not / have to / do / .

_____

5 A French teacher / have to / good / at Maths / be / does not / .

_____

6 good / You / do not / have to / be / at French / .

_____

THE PRONOUN *YOU*

GRAMMAR

Use the pronoun *you* to say something to someone.
You have to work many hours. **You** are a very serious teacher.

You can be singular or plural. The verb does not change. It is the same form.

singular	plural
You are a good teacher. (*you* = 1 person)	**You** are great students (*you* = more than 1 person)

You can also mean *people in general*. In this case, it does not mean any one particular person. This meaning is often used in job adverts.
You have to be kind. (People in general have to be kind.)
There is a job for a fitness instructor. **You** must be fit and healthy.
(People who want to be a fitness instructor must be fit and healthy.)

3 Rewrite the sentences. Use *you* as the subject.

1 He must have three years' experience.

_____

2 She is kind and good with people.

_____

3 We have a university education.

_____

4 They speak Chinese.

_____

5 Altan and Elif speak Turkish.

_____

4 Look back at Reading 2 on page 110. Circle the examples of *you* where it means *people in general*.

JOINING SENTENCES WITH *AND*

Simple sentences

A *simple sentence* has a subject and a verb.

subject verb   *subject verb*
You <u>are</u> friendly. **You** <u>are</u> good with people.

When the subjects and verbs in two sentences are the same, you can join these ideas with *and* in one sentence. You only need the subject once.

You are friendly. ~~You~~ and ~~are~~ good with people.
→ You are friendly **and** good with people.

Compound sentences

When the subjects are different in two simple sentences, you can join these together with *and* in one sentence. This is called a *compound sentence*.

You need both subjects. Put a comma before *and*.

subject   verb   subject   verb
The pay <u>is</u> good. **The job** <u>is</u> interesting.

→ The pay is good. , and The job is interesting.
→ The pay is good, **and** the job is interesting.

It is important to have both simple and compound sentences in your writing. This makes your writing more interesting.

1 Rewrite the simple sentences. If the subjects are the same, join the ideas with *and* in one sentence. If the subjects are different, write one compound sentence with *and*.

1 You must be intelligent. You must be good with people.

_____

2 You have to be healthy. You have to be strong.

_____

3 Football players have to be fit. You are fit.

_____

4 The job is to teach English. You are an English and French teacher.

_____

5 You have to be good at Maths. You have to be friendly.

_____

PLUS

WRITING AN EMAIL

Begin an email with a greeting.

Hi, Ahmad!	Use *Hi* for people you know. Use an exclamation mark to show you are happy or excited.
Erik,	Use a person's first name, followed by a comma for most situations.
Dear Daria,	Use *Dear* for people you do not know very well.

End an email with a closing. Write your name after the closing.

Talk to you soon! *Karel*	Use this expression for people you talk to often.
Love, *Mum*	Use this for close family and friends.
Good luck! *Oliver*	Use this phrase to wish someone good luck.

You can use contractions in informal emails to family and friends.

You do not have to work at weekends. → You **don't** have to work at weekends.

I think you will like this job. → I think **you'll** like this job.

It is in South Korea. → **It's** in South Korea.

I hope you are doing well. → I hope **you're** doing well.

I have found a great job for you. → **I've** found a great job for you.

We do not usually use contractions in academic writing.

2 Rewrite the information as emails with a greeting, contractions and a closing. Then compare your work with a partner.

1 **To:** Allen
   Sentences: I am excited to see you. I think you will like my news!
   From: Max

   _____

   _____

   _____

   _____

2 **To:** Jen
   Sentences: You do not have to worry. I found a job for you. It is in London!
   From: Carmen

   _____

   _____

   _____

   _____

3 To: Chuanwei

Sentences: It is great that you found a job! You will be so happy there.

From: Tao

_____

_____

_____

_____

WRITING TASK

▶ Write an email about a job.

PLAN

1 Look at the job you chose for your partner in the Critical thinking section on page 115. Think of details for the job and fill in the table.

Who is the job for?	
What is the job?	
Where is the job?	
What does he / she need to be good at?	
Why is your friend good for the job?	
What is the pay?	
When does he / she work?	

2 Show the table to your partner. What other details can you use? Add them to the table.

3 Read the Task checklist on page 122 as you prepare your email.

WRITE A FIRST DRAFT

4 Now use the information from your table to write an email to your partner about the job.

To:
From:
Subject:

_____ (Write your greeting)

I hope you're well. I have a great job for you.

(Write sentences about the job with information from Exercise 1. Use *must* and *have to* with adjective phrases.)

_____

_____

_____

_____

_____

_____

_____

_____

_____

_____

_____

_____

_____

_____

_____

_____

Here's the link: www.discoverjobs4you.com

_____ ! (Closing)

_____ (Write your name)

EDIT

5 Use the Task checklist to review your email.

TASK CHECKLIST	✔
Describe the job and explain why it is good for your partner.	
Use adjective phrases to describe the person for the job.	
Use *must* and *have to* to say that something is necessary.	
Use the pronoun *you* and contractions in your email.	
Use a greeting and closing in your email.	

6 Make any necessary changes to your email.

OBJECTIVES REVIEW

1 Check your learning objectives for this unit. Write *3*, *2* or *1* for each objective.

3 = very well   2 = well   1 = not so well

I can ...

watch and understand a video about a mine.   _____

read for detail.   _____

analyze and evaluate opinions.   _____

use adjective phrases.   _____

use *must* and *have to*.   _____

use the pronoun *you*.   _____

join sentences with *and*.   _____

write an email.   _____

write an email about a job.   _____

2 Go to the *Unlock* Online Workbook for more practice with this unit's learning objectives.

UNL⊘CK
ONLINE

WORDLIST

company (n) ⊙	great (adj) ⊙	medicine (n) ⊙
doctor (n) ⊙	gym (n)	nurse (n) ⊙
engineer (n) ⊙	healthy (adj) ⊙	office (n) ⊙
farmer (n) ⊙	high school (n)	pay (n) ⊙
fit (adj) ⊙	hospital (n) ⊙	pilot (n) ⊙
fitness instructor (n)	interesting (adj) ⊙	school (n) ⊙
football player (n)	journalist (n)	school teacher (n)
friendly (adj) ⊙	language teacher (n)	software engineer (n)
good at (adj)	manager (n) ⊙	

⊙ = high-frequency words in the Cambridge Academic Corpus

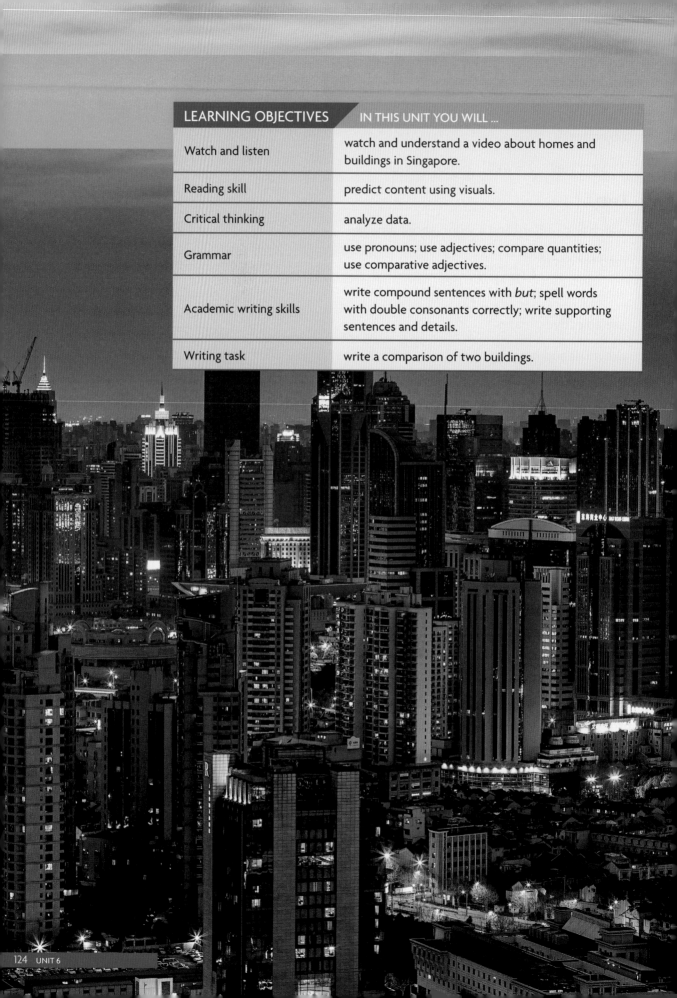

LEARNING OBJECTIVES

IN THIS UNIT YOU WILL ...

Watch and listen	watch and understand a video about homes and buildings in Singapore.
Reading skill	predict content using visuals.
Critical thinking	analyze data.
Grammar	use pronouns; use adjectives; compare quantities; use comparative adjectives.
Academic writing skills	write compound sentences with *but*; spell words with double consonants correctly; write supporting sentences and details.
Writing task	write a comparison of two buildings.

HOMES AND BUILDINGS

UNL⌀CK YOUR KNOWLEDGE

Look at the photo. Ask and answer the questions with a partner.

1 Do you think this city is a nice place to live? Why / Why not?
2 How is this city like or not like your town or city?
3 Do you like being in very big cities? Why / Why not?

PLUS

PREPARING TO WATCH

ACTIVATING YOUR
KNOWLEDGE

1 Work with a partner and answer the questions.

1 Are there a lot of tourists in your town or city? Where do most of them come from?

2 What kind of homes do most people in your city live in (a house, flat, etc.)?

3 What do you know about Singapore? Where is it? Tell your partner what you know.

PREDICTING
CONTENT FROM
VISUALS

2 Match the sentences (1–4) to the pictures from the video.

1 This big city is on an island.

2 Inside these tall buildings there are thousands of flats.

3 The port is always busy.

4 This famous hotel is more than a hundred years old.

GLOSSARY

transport (n) a train, car, bus, ship or plane to get you from one place to another

port (n) a place near the water where ships arrive and leave from

traditional (adj) doing something in the old way

luxury hotel (n) a very expensive and comfortable hotel

own (v) to have; when you own something, it is yours

WHILE WATCHING

3 ▶ Watch the video. Write *T* (True) or *F* (False) next to the statements. Then correct the false statements.

_____ 1 Singapore is an island.

_____

_____ 2 Singapore has the busiest port in the world.

_____

_____ 3 Most people in Singapore live in houses.

_____

_____ 4 Singapore has a lot of hotels.

_____

_____ 5 Most people in Singapore own their homes.

_____

4 ▶ Watch again. Circle the correct word or phrase.

1 Singapore is a centre for *technology / education*.
2 *Space / transport* is a problem in Singapore.
3 A hundred years ago, many people in Singapore lived *on farms / above shops*.
4 About *50% / 80%* of people in Singapore live in tall buildings.
5 Most hotels in Singapore are *traditional / modern*.

5 Complete the sentences with words from the box.

plane   close   home   shopping

1 People live very _____ together in Singapore.
2 People in Singapore can go to school and go _____ near their homes.
3 Most tourists come to Singapore in a car or _____ .
4 Buying a _____ is important in Singapore.

DISCUSSION

6 Work in a small group. Discuss the questions.

1 Would you like to visit Singapore? Why / Why not?
2 How is Singapore like your city? How is it different?
3 Do you live in a house or a flat? What are some good things about each kind of home? What are some bad things?

READING

READING 1

PREPARING TO READ

USING YOUR
KNOWLEDGE

1 You are going to read an interview with an architect (someone who plans and designs buildings). Ask and answer the questions with a partner.

1 What do you like about your home? What do you not like?
2 What kind of home do you want to live in?
3 What makes a home a good place to live?

UNDERSTANDING
KEY VOCABULARY

2 Read the sentences (1–8). Write the words in bold below the photos (a–h).

1 In a **garden**, you grow flowers and plants.
2 Children drink out of **plastic** cups.
3 Cities have **tall** buildings.
4 Tables and chairs are made of **wood**.
5 The **roof** on our house is red.
6 I have a picture on the **wall**.
7 The sun shines through the **window**.
8 Be careful. **Glass** can break.

_____   _____   _____   _____

_____   _____   _____   _____

Predicting content using visuals

Visuals can be photographs, pictures, graphs or charts. You can use the visuals to help you understand the topic of the text.

3 Look at the photos in the text below. Choose the phrases (a–d) to make sentences you agree with.

PREDICTING CONTENT USING VISUALS

I think the buildings in the photos are ...

a exciting.

b easy to build.

c good for people to live in.

d in the same city.

Architect's world

EXPERT INTERVIEW

1 **Professor Michael Chan** *teaches design to architects at the London School of Architecture. He has been at the school for 30 years. Home design is different today than it was 30 years ago. This week, Michael tells us more about new home design around the world.*

architect Michael Chan

Japanese roof house

garden home with plants

mirror house

2 **Architect's world**: What are your favourite home designs?

Michael Chan: I really like Japanese designs. Many people in Japan build interesting houses. For example, the roof house is very **tall** and has a steep[1] **roof**. The **windows** on the roof are different sizes. Inside the house, the rooms are very narrow[2] and the ceilings are very high. It is simple and very small inside.

3 **AW**: What do you think about 'green'[3] homes?

MC: It is very important to build houses which are good for the Earth. My favourite example is a house in Saigon, Vietnam. It is a 'garden home'. This house is in the middle of a busy city, but there are plants everywhere. From the street, people see a tall **garden**. But, in fact, it is a house. There are plants and trees in front of the glass **walls**. There is also a small garden on the roof. You can put chairs and a table there and enjoy tea with your family.

4 **AW**: What do architects use to build houses?

MC: Many architects use **wood**. It keeps your house warm in winter. They also use metal and **glass**. Sometimes they use something different. For example, one architect from Amsterdam put mirrors on every wall of a house. Other architects use glass or even **plastic** for the walls.

[1]**steep** (adj) goes down very quickly and almost straight down
[2]**narrow** (adj) not much space from one side to the other
[3]**green** (adj) something which does not use a lot of energy

WHILE READING

4 Read the text on page 129. Tick (✔) the boxes in the table which are true for the houses.

	windows are different sizes	has glass walls	has a small garden on the roof	rooms are narrow
Japanese roof house				
Vietnamese 'garden home'				

5 Match the sentence halves to make a main idea.

1 Michael Chan likes   **a** metal, wood, glass and plastic.
2 Green architecture is   **b** good for the Earth.
3 Architects make homes out of   **c** unusual and interesting homes.

6 Read the interview again. Write *T* (true) or *F* (false) next to the statements. Correct the false statements.

_____ 1 Professor Chan's favourite home designs are Korean.

_____

_____ 2 The roof house has small and narrow rooms.

_____

_____ 3 Professor Chan says it is important to build more homes in Vietnam.

_____

_____ 4 The 'garden home' is in the centre of a busy city.

_____

_____ 5 Gardens and plants are good for the Earth.

_____

_____ 6 In Amsterdam, many architects put mirrors on the walls.

_____

DISCUSSION

7 Ask and answer the questions with a partner.

1 Which of the homes in the photos on page 129 do you want to live in? Why?

2 What kind of homes are greenest (best for the Earth)?

READING 2

PREPARING TO READ

1 Tell a partner if you agree or disagree with each sentence. Explain why.

1 It's important for the buildings in a city to look interesting.
2 Tall buildings are better than small buildings.
3 It is fun to be high up in a building.

USING YOUR KNOWLEDGE

2 You are going to read an article about skyscrapers. Read the sentences (1–6). Write the words in bold next to the correct definitions (a–f).

1 The car is too **expensive**. I don't have the money to buy it.
2 The **buildings** in my city are made of metal and glass – both the shops and the offices.
3 You can take a **lift** to the top of the building. It is very high!
4 I live in an **apartment** on the fourth floor.
5 How much does this TV **cost**? I can't see the price.
6 This plane ticket to Edinburgh is very **cheap**! I bought it for only £25!

UNDERSTANDING KEY VOCABULARY

a _____ (adj) costing a lot of money
b _____ (n) a structure with walls and a roof, such as a house, school, etc.
c _____ (adj) costing little money
d _____ (n) a set of rooms for someone to live in on one level of a building or house
e _____ (v) to have an amount of money as a price; you must pay that amount to buy something
f _____ (n) a machine which carries people up and down in tall buildings

PLUS

Skyscrapers

What are skyscrapers?

1 Skyscrapers are very tall **buildings**. They are usually more than 300 metres tall. You can see skyscrapers in cities around the world. Many countries build skyscrapers so tourists go there. There are many skyscrapers in Asia, the Middle East, the Americas and Europe. Inside a skyscraper, there are offices, shops, restaurants and **apartments**.

What are some famous skyscrapers?

2 The Empire State Building in New York is a world-famous skyscraper. It has two million visitors every year. It is popular with tourists, but there are taller and more modern skyscrapers in the Middle East and in Asia. The Shanghai World Financial Center, One World Trade Center in New York and the Burj Khalifa in Dubai are taller than the Empire State Building. The Burj Khalifa is taller than the Shanghai World Financial Center and One World Trade Center. One World Trade Center is taller than the Shanghai World Financial Center. One World Trade Center is more modern than the other two buildings. It opened in 2014.

How much money do skyscrapers cost?

3 Skyscrapers are very **expensive**. They cost more money than other buildings. The Burj Khalifa cost $1,500,000,000 to build. It was more expensive than the Shanghai World Financial Center ($850,000,000), but it was **cheaper** than One World Trade Center. One World Trade Center was the most expensive. It cost $3,900,000,000.

What is inside a skyscraper?

4 The Burj Khalifa has 163 floors. This is more than One World Trade Center or the Shanghai World Financial Center. One World Trade Center has 104 floors and the Shanghai World Financial Center has 101 floors. All skyscrapers have **lifts**. The Burj Khalifa has more lifts than One World Trade Center or the Shanghai World Financial Center. It has 57 lifts. One World Trade Center has 54 lifts, but the Shanghai World Financial Center has fewer. It has only 31. Many skyscrapers also have shopping centres or malls inside them. A lot of people come to shop every day.

Shanghai World Financial Center (2008) **492 m**

One World Trade Center (2014) **546 m**

Burj Khalifa (2010) **830 m**

WHILE READING

3 Scan the text on page 132. Write words from the text in the table.

Scan the text on page 132.

SCANNING TO FIND INFORMATION

	Shanghai World Financial Center	One World Trade Center	Burj Khalifa
A city	Shanghai	New York	(1)_____
B height (m)	(2)_____	(3)_____	830
C year	2008	2014	2010
D number of floors	(4)_____	104	163
E number of lifts	(5)_____	54	57
F cost (USD)	$850,000,000	(6)$_____	$1,500,000,000

4 Follow the directions to annotate the text.

READING FOR DETAIL

1 Underline the four questions in italics the text asks.
2 Underline key words in each paragraph which answer the question.
3 Compare your answers with a partner.

DISCUSSION

5 Ask and answer the questions with a partner. Look at the photos and the text.

SYNTHESIZING

1 Which skyscraper was the most expensive to build? Why do you think it was so expensive?
2 How long do you think it takes to build a skyscraper?
3 Use information from Reading 1 and Reading 2 to answer the question: Can skyscrapers be green (good for the Earth)? Why / Why not?

PRONOUNS

GRAMMAR

You can match pronouns to nouns to help you understand a text.

Skyscrapers are very tall buildings. **They** [They = Skyscrapers] are usually more than 300 m tall.

The Empire State Building in New York is a world-famous skyscraper. **It** [It = The Empire State Building] has two million visitors every year.

PLUS

1 Read the text on page 132 again. Match the words and phrases in the box to the pronouns in bold in the sentences (1–4).

> the Burj Khalifa   One World Trade Center
> the Shanghai World Financial Center   skyscrapers

1 **It** was more expensive than the Shanghai World Financial Center ($850,000,000). _____

2 **It** opened in 2014. _____

3 **They** cost more money than other buildings. _____

4 **It** has only 31 lifts. _____

VOCABULARY FOR BUILDINGS

2 Complete the sentences with the words in the box.

> apartments   ceiling   lifts   entrance   exit   garden
> car park   roof   shopping centre   stairs   walls   windows

1 There are over 520 different shops in the Mall of America, which is a _____ in the US.

2 In the Burj Khalifa, there are over 900 _____ you can live in.

3 It is popular for a building to have a _____ on the _____ . The plants on top of the building are good for the city.

4 The John Hancock Center in Chicago has a race up the building. People run up the _____ .

5 Skyscrapers often have one main _____ at the front of the building. It is also the _____ . You leave from there, too.

6 One World Trade Center has 13,000 glass _____ .

7 Each floor in One World Trade Center is 3 m high from floor to _____ .

8 There are 1,100 parking spaces in the _____ at the Shanghai World Financial Center.

9 The _____ of skyscrapers have to be very strong. They hold the building up.

10 Skyscrapers must have _____ . They are too tall for people to walk up the stairs.

3 Read the sentences and circle the correct words.

1 You can leave your car in the *garden / car park*.
2 You can take the *lift / stairs* to the next floor.
3 You go into a building through the *entrance / exit*.
4 You can walk up the *lift / stairs* to the next floor.
5 You must go to the *entrance / exit* to get out if there is a fire.
6 I live in *an apartment / a shopping centre* in the city.
7 I have beautiful pictures on my *ceiling / walls*.
8 The *windows / roof* in my house are made of glass.

PLUS

ADJECTIVES

4 Match the adjectives (1–6) to their opposites (a–f).

1 big	a ugly
2 tall	b cheap
3 traditional	c short
4 old	d small
5 expensive	e modern
6 beautiful	f new

5 Complete the sentences with the adjectives in the box. For some items, more than one answer is possible.

beautiful   cheap   expensive   modern   traditional   ugly

1 It is _____ to build skyscrapers. They are not cheap.
2 Buildings with glass look _____ . They shine in the sun.
3 Skyscrapers are _____ buildings. They are new and interesting.
4 Some homes in China are _____ . They look like homes from the past.
5 It is hard to find a _____ apartment in the city. They cost too much money.
6 Most people like skyscrapers, but I think they are _____ . I prefer small buildings and more traditional designs.

WRITING

CRITICAL THINKING

At the end of this unit, you are going to write a comparison. Look at this unit's writing task in the box below.

> Write a comparison of two buildings.

SKILLS

Analyzing data

Data is information. Data can come in many different forms, but it is often in numbers. When you have data, you need to analyze it – to look at it closely – in order to understand what it is saying.

UNDERSTAND

1 Read the sentences (1–5) and match them with the same data in the table on page 133. Write the letter of the row (A–F) at the end of the sentence it matches. You don't need to use all the rows.

1 The Burj Khalifa cost $1,500,000,000 to build. It was more expensive than the Shanghai World Financial Center ($850,000,000), but it was cheaper than One World Trade Center. One World Trade Center cost $3,900,000,000. _____

2 The Burj Khalifa has 163 floors. This is more than One World Trade Center or the Shanghai World Financial Center. One World Trade Center has 104 floors and the Shanghai World Financial Center has 101 floors. _____

3 The Burj Khalifa has more lifts than One World Trade Center or the Shanghai World Financial Center. It has 57 lifts. One World Trade Center has 54 lifts, but the Shanghai World Financial Center has fewer. It has only 31. _____

4 The Burj Khalifa is 830 metres tall. One World Trade Center is also tall, but not as tall as the Burj Khalifa. It is 546 metres tall. The Shanghai World Financial Center is 492 metres high. _____

5 The Shanghai World Financial Center was built in 2008. They built it before the other buildings. The Burj Khalifa was built in 2010 and One World Trade Center was completed in 2014. _____

2 Compare your answers with a partner. Make changes if necessary.

3 Work with a partner. Choose two skyscrapers you are interested in. Find information on the internet to complete the table. Choose buildings from the box or a different building you like.

APPLY

> Empire State Building   Bank of China Tower
> Taipei 101   Petronas Twin Towers   Burj Al Arab

	_____ (building 1)	_____ (building 2)
city		
height (m)		
year		
number of floors		
number of lifts		
cost		

4 Work with a partner. Ask and answer the questions about your buildings.

ANALYZE

1 Which building is taller?

_____

2 Which building is more modern?

_____

3 Which building has more floors?

_____

4 Which building has more lifts?

_____

5 Which building was more expensive?

_____

GRAMMAR FOR WRITING

COMPARING QUANTITIES

You can compare quantities with *more / fewer / less* + a noun or a noun phrase + *than*. This phrase comes after the subject and the verb.

Use *more* for a higher quantity.

One World Trade Center has **more lifts than** the Shanghai World Financial Center.
Skyscrapers cost **more money than** other buildings.
The garden home in Saigon has **more rooms than** the roof house.

Use *fewer* or *less* for a lower quantity. Use *fewer* with countable nouns (things you can count) and use *less* with uncountable nouns (things you cannot count). You will learn more about countable and uncountable nouns in Unit 7.

The Shanghai World Financial Center has **fewer lifts than** One World Trade Center.
There is **less information** about Building B **than** about Building A.

1 Put the words and phrases in order to make sentences.

1 The Burj Khalifa / more / floors / than Taipei 101 / has / .

_____

2 visitors / than / has / The Burj Khalifa / the Shanghai World Financial Center / more / .

_____

3 more / than the British Museum / The Shard / has / stairs / .

_____

4 has / than the British Museum / lifts / more / The Louvre Museum / .

_____

5 money / cost / One World Trade Center / than the Burj Khalifa / more / .

_____

6 The Burj Khalifa / less / money / cost / than One World Trade Center / .

_____

7 has / lifts / The Shanghai World Financial Center / fewer / than One World Trade Center / .

_____

COMPARATIVE ADJECTIVES

Use comparative adjectives to describe how two things are different.

For one-syllable adjectives, add -(e)r + than.

tall ➔ tall**er** than

The Burj Khalifa is **taller than** the Shanghai World Financial Center.

The roof house is **smaller than** the garden home.

For adjectives with two syllables which end in a consonant + -y, replace the -y with -i and add -er + than.

busy ➔ busi**er than**

Shanghai is **busier than** Cambridge.

For adjectives with two or more syllables, use *more* + adjective + *than* or *less* + adjective + *than*.

expensive ➔ **more** expensive **than** / **less** expensive **than**

One World Trade Center was **more expensive than** the Burj Khalifa.

The Burj Khalifa was **less expensive than** One World Trade Center.

Some comparatives are irregular:

good ➔ **better**   bad ➔ **worse**

My new house is **better than** my old flat.

The traffic in Madrid is **worse than** the traffic in my village.

2 Correct the mistakes in the sentences. Then compare your answers with a partner.

1 The Louvre Museum is more popular the British Museum.

_____

2 The SM Mall of Asia is more of modern the Istanbul Cevahir.

_____

3 The Country Club Plaza is more small the Istanbul Cevahir.

_____

4 Modern buildings are beautifuler than traditional buildings.

_____

5 The Burj Khalifa is tall One World Trade Center.

_____

6 Wood is more expensive that plastic.

_____

7 This street is many busy than the main road.

_____

8 Many buildings in London are more old than buildings in New York.

_____

9 The traffic in the city is more bad than the traffic than in the village.

_____

ACADEMIC WRITING SKILLS

COMPOUND SENTENCES WITH *BUT*

SKILLS

A sentence always has a subject and a verb. You can use *but* to join two simple sentences to make a compound sentence. *But* makes a comparison.

Sentences 1 and 2:

subject   *verb*   *subject*   *verb*

One World Trade Center is tall. The Burj Khalifa is taller than One World Trade Center.

↓

Join sentences 1 and 2 with *but*. Add a comma before *but*:

One World Trade Center is tall, **but** the Burj Khalifa is taller than One World Trade Center.

↓

Do not repeat *than* + noun phrase after a comparison:

One World Trade Center is tall, **but** the Burj Khalifa is taller ~~than One World Trade Center~~.

↓

New sentence:

One World Trade Center is tall, **but** the Burj Khalifa is taller.

---

1 Join each pair of simple sentences below to make one compound sentence with *but*.

1 The Metro Centre has more floors than the Country Club Plaza. The Country Club Plaza has more restaurants than the Metro Centre.

_____

_____

2 The Istanbul Cevahir has more cinemas than the SM Mall of Asia. The SM Mall of Asia has more shops than the Istanbul Cevahir.

_____

_____

3 The Metro Centre is more modern than the Country Club Plaza. The Country Club Plaza is bigger than the Metro Centre.

_____

_____

4 The SM Mall of Asia is bigger than the Country Club Plaza. The Country Club Plaza is older than the SM Mall of Asia.

_____

_____

PLUS

Double consonants

SKILLS

Vowels are the letters *a, e, i, o* and *u*. The other letters in the alphabet are *consonants*: *b, c, d, f,* etc. We sometimes repeat a consonant in some comparative adjectives and some verb forms. If we repeat a consonant, we *double* it.

We double the consonant if:
* the word has one syllable
* the last two letters of the word are a vowel + a consonant
* the last consonant is not *-y*

comparative adjectives: bi**g** → bi**gg**er, fat → fa**tt**er, thin → thi**nn**er
the *-ing* forms of some verbs: swi**m** → swi**mm**ing, run → ru**nn**ing,
sho**p** → sho**pp**ing

2 Read the text below and correct the underlined words. Correct the spelling and/or add any missing capital letters.

What are <u>mals</u>?

Malls are big buildings for <u>shoping</u>. They are near big cities. Sometimes they are inside skyscrapers. Many cities have more than one mall. Malls have <u>restorants</u> and <u>sinemas</u>. The <u>restaraunts</u> are <u>biger</u> than <u>restrants</u> in the city. Some malls also have gyms and <u>swiming</u> pools.

<u>southdale center</u> in <u>minnesota</u> in the <u>united states</u> was the first mall in the world. It is popular today but there are <u>biger</u> malls in <u>america</u>, <u>europe</u>, the <u>gulf</u> and <u>asia</u>.

SUPPORTING SENTENCES

Supporting sentences are in the middle of a paragraph. Supporting sentences give details and examples to make the topic sentence clearer. All supporting sentences should be about the topic sentence.

topic sentence	Skyscrapers are very expensive.
supporting sentences and details	They cost more money than other buildings. The Burj Khalifa cost $1,500,000,000 to build. It was more expensive than the Shanghai World Financial Center ($850,000,000), but it was cheaper than One World Trade Center. One World Trade Center cost $3,900,000,000.

3 Read the topic sentences (1–2). Tick (✔) the supporting sentences and details that explain the topic sentence.

1 **topic sentence:** Skyscrapers are very tall buildings.
_____ They are usually more than 300 metres tall.
_____ The Burj Khalifa has more lifts than One World Trade Center or the Shanghai World Financial Center.
_____ Many countries build skyscrapers, so tourists go there.
_____ There are many skyscrapers in Asia, the Middle East, the Americas and Europe.

2 **topic sentence:** All skyscrapers have lifts.
_____ The Burj Khalifa has more lifts than One World Trade Center or the Shanghai World Financial Center.
_____ It has 57 lifts.
_____ One World Trade Center cost $3,900,000,000.
_____ The Empire State Building in New York is a world-famous skyscraper.
_____ One World Trade Center has 54 lifts, but the Shanghai World Financial Center has fewer.

4 Read the topic sentences (1–2). Find a supporting sentence in Reading 1 or Reading 2 for each topic sentence.

1 **topic sentence:** Skyscrapers are very tall.
supporting sentence:

_____

2 **topic sentence:** It is important to build houses which are good for the Earth.
supporting sentence:

_____

5 Read the topic sentences (1–2). Write a supporting sentence to explain each topic sentence.

1 **topic sentence:** Modern design is interesting.
supporting sentence:

_____

2 **topic sentence:** Skyscrapers are very expensive.
supporting sentence:

_____

WRITING TASK

▶ Write a comparison of two buildings.

PLAN

1 Look at the table you completed in the Critical thinking section on page 137. What other information can you research about your skyscrapers? Write two or more topics to compare in the table. Add the information you find about your buildings.

	(building 1)	(building 2)
_____		
_____		
_____		
_____		

2 Read the Task checklist on page 144 as you prepare your paragraph.

WRITE A FIRST DRAFT

3 Write sentences for each topic. Use the information in your chart from the Critical thinking section and from Exercise 1 on page 143.

   1 Write the names of your buildings. Write what city they are in.
   2 Compare the height of your buildings.
   3 Compare the year your buildings opened.
   4 Compare the number of floors in your buildings.
   5 Compare the number of lifts in your buildings.
   6 Compare the cost of your buildings.
   7 Compare any other information you have.

EDIT

4 Use the Task checklist to review your paragraph.

TASK CHECKLIST	✔
Use supporting sentences and details to explain the topic sentence and compare two different buildings.	
Use pronouns to refer to your buildings.	
Use sentences which compare quantities.	
Make sure sentences have *than* after a comparative adjective.	
Join sentences with *but* to make comparisons.	

5 Make any necessary changes to your paragraph.

OBJECTIVES REVIEW

1 Check your learning objectives for this unit. Write *3, 2* or *1* for each objective.

3 = very well   2 = well   1 = not so well

I can ...

watch and understand a video about homes and buildings in Singapore. _____

predict content using visuals. _____

analyze data. _____

use pronouns. _____

use adjectives. _____

compare quantities. _____

use comparative adjectives. _____

write compound sentences with *but*. _____

spell words with double consonants correctly. _____

write supporting sentences and details. _____

write a comparison of two buildings. _____

2 Go to the *Unlock* Online Workbook for more practice with this unit's learning objectives.

 UNLOCK ONLINE

WORDLIST

apartment (n)	expensive (adj) ⊙	short (adj) ⊙
beautiful (adj) ⊙	garden (n) ⊙	small (adj) ⊙
big (adj) ⊙	glass (n) ⊙	stairs (n) ⊙
building (n) ⊙	lift (n) ⊙	tall (adj) ⊙
car park (n)	modern (adj) ⊙	traditional (adj) ⊙
ceiling (n)	new (adj) ⊙	ugly (adj) ⊙
cheap (adj) ⊙	old (adj) ⊙	wall (n) ⊙
cost (v) ⊙	plastic (adj) ⊙	window (n) ⊙
entrance (n) ⊙	roof (n) ⊙	wood (n) ⊙
exit (n) ⊙	shopping centre (n)	

⊙ = high-frequency words in the Cambridge Academic Corpus

LEARNING OBJECTIVES	IN THIS UNIT YOU WILL ...
Watch and listen	watch and understand a video about goat's cheese.
Reading skill	skim a text; take notes.
Critical thinking	generate ideas.
Grammar	use countable and uncountable nouns; use *can* and *cannot*; use subject–verb agreement; use determiners *a*, *an* and *some*.
Academic writing skills	understand error correction marks; write concluding sentences.
Writing task	write about popular food in your country.

FOOD AND CULTURE

UNLOCK YOUR KNOWLEDGE

Look at the photo. Ask and answer the questions with a partner.

1 What is the woman doing?
2 What foods do you see?
3 What foods do you usually buy?

PLUS

WATCH AND LISTEN

Arreau

PREPARING TO WATCH

ACTIVATING YOUR KNOWLEDGE

1 Work with a partner and answer the questions.

1 What kinds of food come from cows? Which ones do you like?
2 What food is popular in your country?
3 Does your country have a national dish? Describe it.

PREDICTING CONTENT USING VISUALS

2 Look at the pictures from the video. Write the words from the box in the gaps.

> village   farm   fruit   cheese

1 This is a French _____ .
2 Farmers are selling _____ .
3 The goats live on a _____ .
4 The man is making _____ .

GLOSSARY

---

market (n) a place where people go to buy or sell things

quart (n) a unit for measuring liquid, equal to 1.14 litres in the UK and 0.95 litres in the US

ingredient (n) one of the different foods that a particular type of food or dish is made from

turn over (phr v) to flip something over to its opposite side

WHILE WATCHING

3 ▶ Watch the video. Tick (✔) the true statements.

UNDERSTANDING
MAIN IDEAS

1 ☐ The village of Arreau is in the south of France.
2 ☐ The south of France is very rainy.
3 ☐ Cheese is very popular in France.
4 ☐ People can learn how to make cheese at the Tuchans' farm.
5 ☐ They get milk from the goats once a day.
6 ☐ Salt is one of the ingredients in the cheese.
7 ☐ Mrs Tuchan makes the cheese and Mr Tuchan sells it.

4 ▶ Watch again. Answer the questions.

UNDERSTANDING
DETAIL

1 What do farmers sell in the market? _____
2 What does Mrs Tuchan sell? _____
3 Where do the goats wait? _____
4 How much milk can a goat make every day? _____
5 Where does Mr Tuchan put the cheese? _____
6 How long does the cheese stay in the room? _____

5 Match the sentence halves.

MAKING INFERENCES

1 The farmers have to   a like cheese.
2 Making cheese   b have traditional foods.
3 Most French people   c look after the goats.
4 Most countries   d takes time.

DISCUSSION

6 Ask and answer the questions with a partner.

1 What do you think is interesting or surprising about making goat's cheese?
2 What kinds of food or other things can you buy in outdoor markets in your country?
3 Why are traditional foods important?

READING

PREPARING TO READ

1 Ask and answer the questions with a partner.

1 What foods are popular all over the world?
2 Why do you think those foods are popular?
3 What are your favourite foods? Why?

2 You are going to read an article about tea. Read the sentences (1–7). Write the words in bold next to the correct definitions (a–g).

1 I enjoy a cup of tea in the afternoon. I add **honey** to make it sweet.
2 I can play many **different** sports. I like football, basketball and tennis.
3 My father **prepares** our family's dinner at the weekends. He really likes cooking.
4 We buy our **bread** at a bakery. I enjoy it with butter and jam.
5 I have the **same** colour eyes as my mother. They are dark grey.
6 There are five main **types** of food: grains, meats, fruits, vegetables and dairy.
7 When it is hot outside, it is good to have water or other **drinks**.

a _____ (n) a basic food made from flour, water and salt mixed together and baked
b _____ (adj) like something else
c _____ (adj) not like other things
d _____ (n) a group of things which are like each other
e _____ (n) a sweet and sticky food made by bees
f _____ (n) liquids that you can put in your mouth and swallow, like water or juice
g _____ (v) to make something

SKILLS

Skimming

If you look for the main topic and idea of a text, you are *skimming*. When you skim, do not read every word. Read the nouns, verbs, adjectives and question words.

3 Read the blue words in the texts on page 152. Write *T* (true) or *F* (false) next to the statements. Correct the false statements.

SKIMMING

_____ 1 The texts compare tea and coffee.

_____

_____ 2 Tea is popular in many countries.

_____

_____ 3 There is one kind of tea.

_____

_____ 4 The text talks about different ways that people prepare tea.

_____

4 Write the paragraph number (1–7) from the text next to the correct main idea (a–e). You will not use all the paragraphs.

READING FOR
MAIN IDEAS

_____ a People use special kettles to prepare tea.
_____ b The history of tea started in Asia.
_____ c There are different kinds of tea made from tea leaves.
_____ d In Kuala Lumpur, pulled tea is special.
_____ e Tea is very popular.

Tea: a world history

by A. Capper

INTRODUCTION: THE WORLD IN A TEACUP

1 Tea is tasty and good for you. It is also one of the most popular **drinks** around the world. But what is tea? And why is it so popular?

2 All tea comes from tea leaves, but tea is not always the **same**. There are many kinds of tea. You can drink black tea, green tea, white tea or fruit tea. Each **type** of tea has a **different** taste and a different colour.

1.1 a tea seller prepares tea in Kuala Lumpur

3 The history of tea begins in Asia. In China, Korea and Japan, tea is still very important today. In Japan, it can take many hours to **prepare** and drink tea with your guests. In Malaysia, a popular drink at breakfast is *teh tarik* ('pulled tea'). Malaysians say it is good for you and tastes good with *roti canai* – a kind of **bread**.

4 Tourists in Kuala Lumpur like watching the tea sellers make 'pulled tea'. The tea sellers pour hot water on black tea. After five minutes, they add sugar and milk. Then they 'pull' the tea – they pour the tea from one cup to another many times.

5 In many countries, you must have a special kettle[1] to make tea. People in different countries also like to add different things to their tea. For example, Russians use a special kettle called a *samovar*. They like drinking tea with lemon. Sometimes, they also drink tea with some sugar or jam. This makes it sweet.

1.2 a Russian samovar

6 In Turkey, tea comes in a *Çaydanlık*. A *Çaydanlık* has two kettles: one for the water and one for the tea. Drink Turkish tea with some sugar.

7 Arab tea, called *karak*, is made with cardamom[2], ginger, milk and sugar. In the United Kingdom, they add some milk and sugar. The British usually eat biscuits with their tea. In the United States, tea is popular with **honey**.

1.3 a Turkish Çaydanlık set

[1]**kettle** (n) a container with a lid and a handle for boiling water
[2]**cardamom** (n) a South Asian plant with seeds used as a spice

Taking notes

When you take notes, you write down the important information from the text. You do not need to write complete sentences. You can use a table to organize your ideas.

5 Write information from the text in the table.

country	How is the tea prepared? What do people eat with it?
Malaysia	1 Pour hot water on black tea. • After five minutes, add sugar and milk. • Then 'pull' the tea. (Pour the tea from one cup to another many times.) • Eat *roti canai* with it.
Russia	2
Turkey	3
Arab countries	4
United Kingdom	5

6 Scan the text. Write the names of the correct countries from the text in the gaps.

1 People in _____ drink *teh tarik*.
2 In _____ , people prepare tea in a *samovar*.
3 People prepare tea with two kettles in _____ .
4 Tourists like watching tea sellers prepare tea in _____ .

DISCUSSION

7 Ask and answer the questions with a partner.

1 How do people drink tea in your country? (With sugar? With milk?)
2 Why do you think tea is a popular drink around the world?

PREPARING TO READ

USING YOUR
KNOWLEDGE

1 Work with a partner. Write different types of food in the table. Describe the food to your partner.

What foods do you like to eat in restaurants?	What foods do you like from your country?	What foods do you like from other countries?

PREVIEWING

2 You are going to read a web article. Look at the text and the photos on page 156. Circle the correct options.

1 The text is from a website for *tourists / students*.
2 The text is about different *types of food / things to do* in Melbourne.

UNDERSTANDING
KEY VOCABULARY

3 Read the sentences (1–5). Match the words in bold to the photos (a–e).

1 I eat **meat** for dinner. I like burgers or steak. _____
2 I buy **vegetables** at the market in my city. _____
3 My dad is a fisherman, so we eat a lot of **fish**. _____
4 In Mexico, beans and **rice** are popular. _____
5 I eat three **meals** a day: breakfast, lunch and dinner. _____

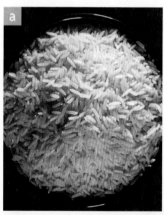

4 Read the sentences (1–2). Write the words in bold next to the correct definitions (a–b).

1 Restaurants in the UK often **serve** fish **with** chips.
2 A popular **dish** for breakfast in the United States is pancakes.

_____ a (n) food that is prepared in a particular way as part of a meal
_____ b (v phr) to give someone food with other food on the same plate or as part of the same meal

WHILE READING

5 Scan the text on page 156. Write *T* (true) or *F* (false) next to the statements. Correct the false statements.

_____ 1 The different cuisines are in alphabetical order.
_____

_____ 2 *Shawarma* is a fish dish.
_____

_____ 3 *Amok trey* is an Australian dish.
_____

_____ 4 You cannot get kangaroo meat in Australian restaurants.
_____

_____ 5 Meat is popular in Arab cuisine.
_____

_____ 6 There are different types of *kabsa*.
_____

_____ 7 Kangaroo burgers are served on rice.
_____

6 Read the questions. Underline the key words in the text. Then write the answers to the questions.

1 Where is *kabsa* a very popular dish?
_____

2 Which dishes are served in or on bread?
_____

3 Which kinds of meat are good for you?
_____

4 Which cuisines have rice dishes?
_____

5 Which cuisines have fish dishes?
_____

SCANNING TO FIND INFORMATION

READING FOR DETAIL

Melbourne/Student Guide

Home | The city | Map | Public transport | Culture | Entertainment | Help

VOTED THE BEST ONLINE CITY GUIDE BY STUDY AUSTRALIA

10

Arab cuisine

Australian cuisine

American cuisine

Cambodian cuisine

Chinese cuisine

French cuisine

Japanese cuisine

Korean cuisine

Mexican cuisine

Turkish cuisine

OF THE BEST BY CUISINE

Melbourne is a big city. We have cuisines from all over the world. Try some!

kabsa

crocodile

amok trey

Arab cuisine[1]

1 At an Arab restaurant, you can find delicious **meat dishes**. Two popular dishes are *shawarma* and *kabsa*. *Shawarma* is a savoury[2] meat dish. The meat is served in *pita* bread with **vegetables**. *Kabsa* is a popular **meal** in many Arab countries and it is very popular in Saudi Arabia. *Kabsa* is a dish with **rice**, meat and vegetables. There are many different ways to prepare *kabsa*. It can be served with onions, chillies and other spices. If you like meat dishes, you will enjoy your meal at an Arab restaurant.

2 In addition to the many flavourful meat dishes, you can get many delicious vegetable dishes.

Read more

Australian cuisine

3 If you are in Australia, you must try a crocodile or kangaroo dish! Many Australian restaurants serve crocodile curry. Crocodile meat is tasty and very good for you. (It is better that you eat crocodile than a crocodile eats you!) Kangaroo meat is also good for you. Kangaroo burgers are served on a type of bread. Australian restaurants also serve great fish and many other dishes.

Read more

Cambodian cuisine

4 At a Cambodian restaurant, there are many types of dish. Cambodians like **fish** with rice. Cambodian dishes are **served with** a lot of vegetables. They are very popular in Cambodian cuisine. One famous dish is *amok trey*. Cambodians prepare *amok trey* with fish, nuts, coconut milk and egg. There are many tasty dishes, but this is one of the best.

Read more

[1]**cuisine** (n) a style of cooking
[2]**savoury** (adj) food which is salty or spicy and not sweet

DISCUSSION

7 Ask and answer the questions with a partner.

1. What dishes do you want to try from Reading 2? Why?
2. What is your favourite meal? Describe the different dishes.
3. Use information from Reading 1 and Reading 2 to answer the following question: Why do different countries have special ways of preparing food and drinks?

⊙ LANGUAGE DEVELOPMENT

VOCABULARY FOR FOOD AND DRINK

1 Write the words from the box under the correct photos. Use the glossary on page 200 to help you.

> rice   dates   milk   honey   onion   chillies   spices
> jam   almonds   yoghurt   water   coconuts

1

_____

2

_____

3

_____

4

_____

5

_____

6

_____

7

_____

8

_____

9

_____

10

_____

11

_____

12

_____

2 Work with a partner. Write the names of food next to each description. Use your own ideas and look at the pictures from Exercise 3 on page 154, Reading 2 on page 156 and Exercise 1 on page 157 to help you.

description	food
sweet	
savoury	
good for you	
popular	

3 Look at the foods you have listed. With a partner, discuss how they are prepared and what they are usually served with.

COUNTABLE AND UNCOUNTABLE NOUNS

Countable nouns name things you can count, such as vegetables, drinks and meals. They can have a singular or a plural form and a singular or a plural verb.

singular	plural
One **vegetable is** cabbage.	**Vegetables are** served in *pita* bread.
A popular **dish is** *shawarma*.	Two popular **dishes are** *shawarma* and *kabsa*.

Uncountable nouns are words for things that you cannot count, like meat, rice and honey. They have a singular form and a singular verb. They do not have a plural form or a plural verb.

Meat is good for you. ~~Meats are good for you.~~
Rice is served with many dishes. ~~Rices are served with many dishes.~~

4 Read the sentences. Tick (✔) if they are correct and put a cross (✘) if they are incorrect. Use a dictionary to help you. Correct the incorrect sentences.

_____ 1 Honeys are sweet.

    _____

_____ 2 Vegetables are popular in European cuisine.

    _____

_____ 3 Milks are good for children.

    _____

_____ 4 Fishes are tasty.

    _____

_____ 5 They serve biscuits with tea.

    _____

_____ 6 Waters are served in a glass.

    _____

5 Look back at Exercise 1 on page 157. Write *C* (countable) or *U* (uncountable) next to the nouns and photos.

CAN AND CANNOT

Use *can* + infinitive to show that an action is possible. Use *cannot* + infinitive to show that an action is not possible.

You **can get** many delicious vegetable dishes. The dishes **can be** spicy. I **cannot eat** spicy food. I do not feel well afterwards.

The singular and plural forms of *can / cannot* are the same.

I **can**, they **can**, etc.

6 Read the sentences and correct the mistakes in the underlined parts. Check your answers with a partner.

1 A meat dish <u>can has</u> vegetables.

    _____

2 You <u>cannot smelling</u> the food.

    _____

3 Russian tea <u>cans come</u> with jam.

    _____

4 Some people <u>cannot to eat</u> meat.

    _____

5 Chillies <u>can is</u> very spicy.

    _____

WRITING

At the end of this unit, you are going to write about food. Look at this unit's writing task in the box below.

> Write about popular food in your country.

SKILLS

Generating ideas

Thinking about what you want to say or write can sometimes be difficult. When you want to generate ideas, you can use an ideas map. You can think of ideas on your own or in a group. To make an ideas map, you can identify supporting information for a main topic. Look at the ideas map below.

 UNDERSTAND

1 Work with a partner. Write words to describe the dish in the ideas map. Explain what it is made of, tastes like and is served with. Look at Reading 2 on page 156 to help you.

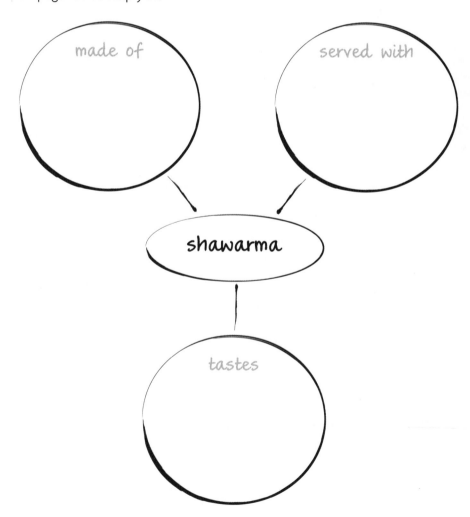

made of

served with

shawarma

tastes

2 Work in small groups. List popular dishes from your country.

REMEMBER

_____

_____

_____

_____

3 Choose two popular dishes from Exercise 2. Write the name of the dish in the middle of each ideas map. Say what each dish is made of, tastes like and is served with.

ANALYZE

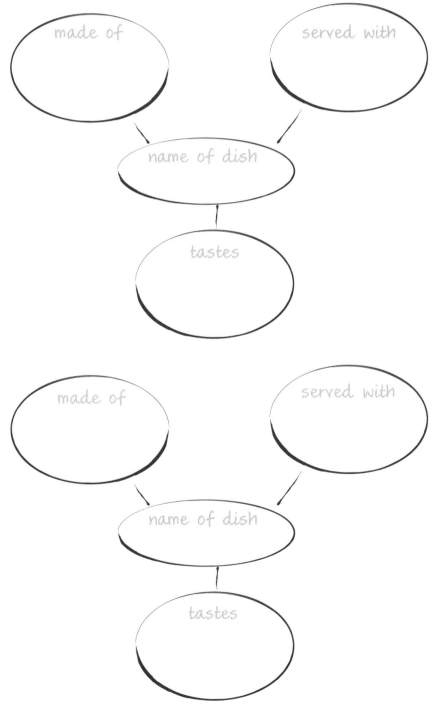

SUBJECT–VERB AGREEMENT

GRAMMAR

A sentence must have a *subject* and a *verb*. The subject can be singular or plural. The verb must agree with the subject.

Use a singular verb form with a singular subject.

subject   *verb*
This **yoghurt**   **is** tasty.

subject   *verb*
It   **is** a popular dish.

subject   *verb*
Vietnamese cuisine   **uses** coconut milk.

Use a plural verb form with a plural subject.

subject   *verb*
The **almonds**   **are** tasty.

subject   *verb*
They   **are** popular dishes.

subject   *verb*
Many dishes   **use** coconut milk.

Remember: Uncountable nouns must have a singular verb form.

1 Circle the correct verb forms.

   1 Turkish chefs *prepare / prepares* small dishes called *meze*.
   2 Latin American cuisine *use / uses* a lot of vegetables.
   3 A famous dish in Japan *is / are* sushi.
   4 Rice *is / are* popular in many restaurants in Korea.
   5 Chinese food *is / are* served with rice and vegetables.
   6 Two popular rice dishes in Thailand *is / are* called *khao mok kai* and *khao na pet*.

2 Read the sentences. Tick (✔) if they are correct and put a cross (✘) if they are incorrect. Use a dictionary to help you.

_____ 1 Korean restaurants serves rice with meat and vegetables.

_____ 2 Butter is served with bread.

_____ 3 Latin American chefs uses many different kinds of vegetables in their dishes.

_____ 4 Kangaroo burgers is served on a type of bread.

_____ 5 Apples and bananas are sweet.

_____ 6 French vegetable soup are delicious.

3 Correct the incorrect sentences in Exercise 2.

1 _____

2 _____

3 _____

4 _____

5 _____

6 _____

DETERMINERS: *A, AN* AND *SOME*

Determiners are words before a noun, such as articles (*a*, *an*, *the* and 'the zero article') and other words, such as *some*.

Write articles before a noun or noun phrase.

Use the articles *a* or *an* before a singular countable noun. Use *a* before a consonant sound. Use *an* before a vowel sound.

A famous dish from Italy is *risotto*. Amok trey is **a p**opular Cambodian dish. Jambalaya is **an** American dish. **An a**pple is served with this dish.

Do not use *a / an* before an uncountable noun.

~~Add a honey to the dish. English people drink tea with a milk.~~

Add honey to the dish. English people drink tea with milk.

You can use *some* before:

• a plural countable noun (e.g. vegetables, drinks)
• an uncountable noun (e.g. milk, rice)

Some means 'more than one' before a countable noun.

Some biscuits are served with the coffee. Chefs prepare the dish with **some vegetables**.

Some means 'a (small) part of' before an uncountable noun.

Add **some honey** to the dish. English people drink tea with **some milk**.

4 Correct the underlined parts of the sentences.

1 At <u>some Arab restaurant</u>, you can find delicious meat dishes.

_____

2 The curry is served with <u>a rice</u>.

_____

3 <u>Some famous dish</u> in New Orleans <u>is</u> *jambalaya* and *gumbo*.

_____

4 French chefs add <u>a apple</u> to this dish.

_____

5 Korean chefs prepare many dishes with <u>a meat</u>.

_____

6 <u>Australian</u> like eating <u>a crocodile meat</u>.

_____

7 There are <u>some vegetable</u> in Korean *kimchi*.

_____

8 <u>Some popular dish</u> in Latin America is chicken soup.

_____

ACADEMIC WRITING SKILLS

ERROR CORRECTION

Some teachers use correction codes for errors. Look at the examples below.

[G] = grammar ~~Honey are sweet.~~ → Honey **is** sweet.

[MW] = missing word ~~I drink tea sugar.~~ → I drink tea **with** sugar.

[P] = punctuation ~~I like almonds~~ → I like almonds.

[SP] = spelling mistake ~~They are delicus.~~ → They are **delicious**.

[CL] = capital letter ~~It is an arab dish.~~ → It is an **Arab** dish.

[C] = content (is the information correct?) ~~Amok trey is from France.~~ →
Amok trey is from **Cambodia**.

[WP] = wrong preposition ~~They are served for bread.~~ → They are served
with bread.

1 Look at a student's paragraph marked with correction codes. Correct the mistakes.

> My favourite <u>cusine</u> [SP] ¹_____ is Mexican food. The dishes
> [MW] ²_____ served with rice and beans. They are also served
> <u>of</u> [WP] ³_____ chips and salsa. Salsa is made with tomatoes
> and other vegetables. It can <u>is</u> [G] ⁴_____ spicy. I drink
> <u>mexican</u> [CL] ⁵_____ coffee after my meal. It has cinnamon
> in <u>it</u> [P] ⁶_____ I like all the dishes in this cuisine.

PLUS

CONCLUDING SENTENCES

A *concluding sentence* ends a paragraph. Often it repeats the main idea of the paragraph using different words.

topic sentence + supporting sentences

All tea comes from tea leaves, but tea is not always the same. There are many types of tea. You can drink black tea, green tea, white tea or fruit tea.

concluding sentence

Each type of tea has a different taste and a different colour.

In the example above, the last sentence is the concluding sentence. It repeats the main idea that tea is not always the same.

2 Read the first sentence of the paragraphs. Then tick (✔) the concluding sentence.

1 At a Cambodian restaurant, there are many types of dish.
_____ One famous dish is *amok trey*.
_____ Cambodians prepare *amok trey* with fish, nuts, coconut milk and egg.
_____ There are many tasty dishes, but this is one of the best.
_____ The coconut milk makes it sweet.

2 At an Arab restaurant, you can find delicious meat dishes.
_____ *Shawarma* is a savoury meat dish.
_____ *Kabsa* is a dish with rice, meat and vegetables.
_____ If you like meat dishes, you will enjoy your meal at an Arab restaurant.
_____ *Kabsa* is a popular meal in many Arab countries and it is very popular in Saudi Arabia.

3 Read the paragraphs. Then write a concluding sentence.

1 France is known for its great bakeries. You can get delicious bread, biscuits and other sweet food at these shops. The French are also known for their tasty cheeses. A popular meal is bread and cheese.

_____

_____

2 Brazilian restaurants serve delicious meat dishes. The meat is cooked over a fire and salted. You eat it with vegetables. You can find this savoury dish at most restaurants.

_____

_____

> Write about popular food in your country.

PLAN

1 Look at the brainstorming notes you made in your ideas map in the Critical thinking section on page 161.

2 Think of any more information you would like to add to your ideas map.

3 Read the Task checklist below as you prepare your paragraphs.

WRITE A FIRST DRAFT

4 Follow the instructions to write a paragraph about each dish.

1 Say what dishes are popular in your country.

2 Describe the taste of the first dish. Describe what the dish is made of. Explain what the dish is served in or served with.

3 Describe the taste of the second dish. Describe what the dish is made of. Explain what the dish is served in or served with.

4 Write a concluding sentence to each paragraph.

EDIT

5 Use the Task checklist to review your paragraphs.

TASK CHECKLIST	✔
Write a paragraph about each dish.	
Make sure subjects and verbs agree in your sentences.	
Use the article *a / an* before a singular countable noun.	
Use *some* before a plural countable noun or an uncountable noun.	
End each paragraph with a concluding sentence.	

6 Make any necessary changes to your paragraphs.

OBJECTIVES REVIEW

1 Check your learning objectives for this unit. Write *3, 2* or *1* for each objective.

3 = very well   2 = well   1 = not so well

I can …

watch and understand a video about goat's cheese.   ———

skim a text.   ———

take notes.   ———

generate ideas.   ———

use countable and uncountable nouns.   ———

use *can* and *cannot*.   ———

use subject–verb agreement.   ———

use determiners *a*, *an* and *some*.   ———

understand error correction marks.   ———

write concluding sentences.   ———

write about popular food in my country.   ———

2 Go to the *Unlock* Online Workbook for more practice with this unit's learning objectives.

WORDLIST		
almond (n)	fish (n) ⊙	rice (n) ⊙
bread (n) ⊙	honey (n)	same (adj) ⊙
chilli (n)	jam (n)	serve with (v phr)
coconut (n)	meal (n) ⊙	spice (n)
date (n) ⊙	meat (n) ⊙	type (n) ⊙
different (adj) ⊙	milk (n)	vegetable (n)
dish (n)	onion (n)	water (n) ⊙
drink (n) ⊙	prepare (v) ⊙	yoghurt (n)

⊙ = high-frequency words in the Cambridge Academic Corpus

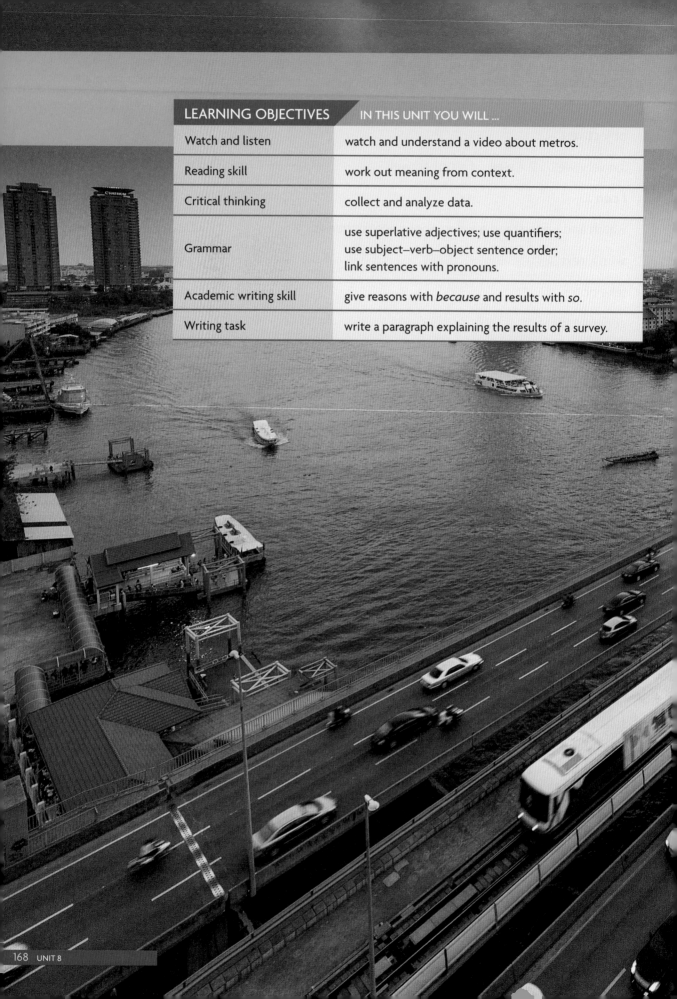

LEARNING OBJECTIVES

IN THIS UNIT YOU WILL ...

Watch and listen	watch and understand a video about metros.
Reading skill	work out meaning from context.
Critical thinking	collect and analyze data.
Grammar	use superlative adjectives; use quantifiers; use subject–verb–object sentence order; link sentences with pronouns.
Academic writing skill	give reasons with *because* and results with *so*.
Writing task	write a paragraph explaining the results of a survey.

TRANSPORT

UNL⊘CK YOUR KNOWLEDGE

Look at the photo. Ask and answer the questions with a partner.

1 How do people in this city get to work and school?
2 Which way looks the fastest? Why?
3 How do you travel to get to work and school? Why?

PREPARING TO WATCH

ACTIVATING YOUR
KNOWLEDGE

1 Work with a partner and answer the questions.

   1 What are the most common types of transport in your city?
   2 What are some unusual types of transport?
   3 What cities have underground or metro systems?

PREDICTING
CONTENT USING
VISUALS

2 Look at the pictures from the video. Circle the correct word.

   1 This train is *underground / overground*.
   2 Many people are waiting to get *on / off* the train.
   3 The city is *busy / quiet*.
   4 The man is helping people in the *shopping centre / metro station*.

GLOSSARY

passenger (n) someone who is travelling in a vehicle, but not controlling the vehicle

platform (n) the area in a train or metro station where you get on and off a train

attendant (n) someone whose job is to help people in a particular place

calm (adj) relaxed; not worried or excited

WHILE WATCHING

UNDERSTANDING
MAIN IDEAS

3 ▶ Watch the video. Write *T* (true) or *F* (false) next to the statements. Correct the false statements.

   _____ 1 Every day, millions of people travel on trains which are under the ground.

   _____

   _____ 2 The oldest underground system is in Tokyo.

   _____

   _____ 3 London's underground system is called the 'Tube'.

   _____

   _____ 4 London has the busiest underground system.

   _____

   _____ 5 Attendants help keep passengers safe, calm and on time.

   _____

4 ▶ Watch again. Choose the correct answer.

1 How many underground systems are there in the world today?
   a over 500
   b over 250
   c over 150

2 How do 500,000 Londoners get to work each day?
   a They go by underground.
   b They walk.
   c They drive.

3 How many people take the Tokyo underground system every hour?
   a 3,500
   b 35,000
   c 350,000

4 Which sentence is not true about Tokyo?
   a There are more people in Tokyo than any other city.
   b There are no underground attendants.
   c There are 8 million passengers on Tokyo's underground every day.

5 Complete the sentences with the words in the box.

| faster | helpful | traffic | usually |

1 There is less _____ on the streets when people take the underground.
2 If you work in a city, the underground is often _____ than a car.
3 People in Tokyo are _____ on time for work.
4 It is _____ to have an attendant on the underground platform.

DISCUSSION

6 Ask and answer the questions with a partner.

1 Have you travelled on the underground in London, Tokyo, New York or another large city? How was it?
2 Underground systems help people in cities like London and Tokyo get to work. What are some other good things about underground systems in cities?
3 What do you think are the easiest ways to travel in a city? Why?

READING

PREPARING TO READ

1 You are going to read about transport. Work with a partner. Look at the text on page 173 and answer the questions.

   1 What type of text is this?
   2 Why do people write this type of text?

2 Read the sentences (1–8). Choose the correct definitions (a or b) for the words in bold.

   1 In cities, there are many options for **transport**. You can take a bus, car or train to work.
      a the things people use to move from one place to another
      b the people living in a certain area
   2 The **traffic** is moving slowly. There are a lot of cars on the road.
      a the cars, trucks, etc. driving on the road
      b the time it takes to get somewhere
   3 When does the **train** get into the station? I need to be there by 9 am.
      a a long, thin type of transport which travels on metal tracks and carries people or things
      b a route or way for travelling from one place to another
   4 I take the **metro** to work. I only have to go two stops.
      a a place for people to walk along the road
      b trains which travel underground, usually in a city
   5 Many children learn to ride a **bicycle**. It's a fun and easy way to travel.
      a a type of transport with two wheels that you sit on and move by pushing two pedals with your feet
      b a type of transport with four wheels and an engine
   6 I took a **taxi** from the airport to the city. It was really expensive!
      a a place for planes to land and people to get on planes
      b a car with a driver who you pay to take you somewhere
   7 My son takes the **bus** to school with other children from his class.
      a a big type of car which carries many passengers by road
      b a small car with three wheels
   8 I don't ride a **motorbike** where I live. It is rainy and I don't want to get wet.
      a a type of transport with two wheels and an engine
      b railway tracks for moving things

We are a group of Engineering students from Australia. This summer, we are studying at Bangkok University of Science and Technology. We would like to find out:

1 how people in Bangkok travel.
2 how people feel about **transport** in Bangkok.

Please answer the questions below. The survey takes about five minutes.

Tick (✔) the correct boxes to answer the questions.

A. About you

A1 Age: How old are you?
☐ 14–17 ☐ 18–21 ☐ 22–31
✔ 32–53 ☐ older than 53

A2 Gender: I am: ☐ male ✔ female

A3 Occupation: What do you do?
☐ study ✔ work

B. Travel

B1 How long is your journey to work or school?
☐ 5–15 minutes ✔ 15–45 minutes
☐ 45–60 minutes ☐ more than 1 hour

B2 How do you get to work or school?
☐ on foot[2] ☐ **bicycle** ☐ car ☐ tuk-tuk
☐ **motorbike** ☐ water taxi ☐ **taxi**
☐ Sky**Train** ✔ **metro** ☐ **bus**

B3 How often do you use these kinds of transport?

Table 1

kinds of transport	always	often	sometimes	not often	never
on foot	✓				
bicycle				✓	
car		✓			
motorbike					✓
water taxi				✓	
taxi				✓	
bus			✓		
SkyTrain			✓		
metro		✓			
tuk-tuk			✓		

B4 Which type or types of transport do you own?
I own a: ☐ bicycle ✔ car ☐ motorbike
☐ other (Please write.): _____

C. Opinion

C1 Read the statements in the table. Do you agree or disagree with them?

Table 2

statements	strongly agree	agree	neither agree nor disagree	disagree	strongly disagree
There is a lot of **traffic** in Bangkok.	✓				
The traffic makes me late.		✓			
We need more public transport.	✓				

C2 Write any comments or suggestions that you have about transport in Bangkok.

We should create more metro lines.
Then more people could use the metro,
and there would not be so much traffic
on the roads.

tuk-tuk   SkyTrain   water taxi

[1] **survey** (n) a set of questions people are asked to get information
[2] **on foot** (prep phr) if you go somewhere on foot, you walk there.

Thank you for taking the time to answer the questions in this survey.

WHILE READING

3 Skim the text. What information is the survey asking about? Circle the correct topics below.

1 the number of hours people in Bangkok work or study
2 how people travel in Bangkok
3 the cost of transport in Bangkok
4 popular forms of transport in Bangkok
5 how people in Bangkok travel on holiday
6 what forms of transport people own

4 Scan the text for the survey answers.

1 How old is the person?

_____

2 How long is the person's journey?

_____

3 How does the person travel to work?

_____

4 What does the person never use for transport?

_____

5 Does the person think the traffic makes her late?

_____

5 Look at the text again. Write T (true) or F (false) next to the statements. Correct the false statements.

_____ 1 There is not a place for people to write their suggestions in the survey.

_____

_____ 2 The survey asks if the person is male or female.

_____

_____ 3 The purpose of the survey is to see how people like Bangkok.

_____

_____ 4 The person answering the survey often takes the bus.

_____

_____ 5 The person answering the survey thinks more water taxis should be added.

_____

READING BETWEEN THE LINES

SKILLS

Working out meaning from context

The type of text and the topic are part of the *context* of a text. The context is also the phrases and sentences in a text which help you understand the meaning of new words.

6 Match the highlighted words in the text on page 173 to their definitions (1–5).

1 another word for *job* _____

2 another word for *questionnaire* _____

3 another word for *on foot* _____

4 another word for *form* or *type* _____

5 a word that means *man* or *woman* _____

WORKING OUT MEANING FROM CONTEXT

DISCUSSION

7 Ask and answer the questions with a partner.

1 What type of transport do people usually use in your city or town?

2 Which types of transport are the best and which are the worst for:

   a long journeys?

   b getting fit and healthy?

   c places with no roads?

   d families?

PREPARING TO READ

USING YOUR
KNOWLEDGE

1 You are going to read a report about transport in Bangkok. A report is a description of something or information about something. Work with a partner to complete the table with ideas.

report	information
weather report	information about ...
news report	information about ...
	information about ...

PREVIEWING

2 Look at the text and the pie chart on page 178. Answer each question (1–3) by choosing the correct option (a–c).

1 What type of text is it?
   a a news report
   b a report for a university class
   c an email to the writer's family
2 What is the main topic of this text?
   a weather
   b food
   c transport
3 Who wrote this text?
   a a student
   b a teacher
   c a journalist

3 Read the definitions. Write the correct form of the words in bold to complete the sentences.

> **drive** (v) to make a car, bus or train move, and control what it does
> **prefer** (v) to like someone or something more than another person or thing
> **report** (n) information about an event or situation
> **result** (n) information which you get from something, like an exam, a survey, a medical test, etc.
> **ride** (v) to travel by sitting on a bike or motorbike, in a bus or metro, etc.
> **spend** (v) to use time by doing something
> **take** (v) to travel somewhere using a taxi, bus or train

1 I _____ riding my bike to going by car. I like to be outside.
2 My mum _____ the bus to work every day. She gets there in ten minutes.
3 My dad _____ 40 minutes in traffic every morning. Driving in the morning takes a lot of time.
4 The traffic _____ said that traffic was moving slowly all over the city.
5 I got the _____ back from my test. I did really well!
6 The bus driver _____ too fast! He should go more slowly on these busy streets.
7 I _____ my motorbike into the city on the weekends. It's faster than my bike.

PLUS

4 Scan the text. Write the correct numbers in the gaps on the pie chart (Figure 1).

Student Name: **Lamal Tongduan**
Student ID: **100035478 / Bangkok University of Science and Technology**
Course: **Transport and the City**

Transport in Bangkok: Report

1 This **report** shows the **results** of a survey about transport in Bangkok. Over 8 million people live in the city. The pie chart (Figure 1) shows the most popular types of transport in Bangkok. It shows the percentage[1] of people who use each type of transport to get to work or school.

2 Every day, thousands of people use public and private transport. A popular form of public transport is the SkyTrain. People take public transport so they don't have to drive themselves. 21% of the population of Bangkok takes the SkyTrain to work or school. Another form of public transport in the city is the bus. 18% of people who live in Bangkok **take** buses. People **prefer** buses to tuk-tuks because buses cost less money. Only 8% of people use tuk-tuks to get to work or school. Most people in Bangkok use private transport. They **drive** their own cars. 14% of people **ride** motorbikes to get to work or take children to school. Only 3% walk to work and only 2% cycle to work. Most places of work are too far away to walk or cycle to so these are the least popular ways to get to work.

3 There is a lot of traffic in Bangkok. The roads are full of different types of vehicles[2] (cars, motorbikes, tuk-tuks, etc.). 23% of people drive a car to work or school. Most people **spend** more than one hour every day travelling because the traffic is so bad. Almost 35% of people are late because of traffic jams. However, there are no traffic jams on the river. 11% of people take the water taxi. It is one of the fastest means of transport.

[1]**percentage** (n) how many out of 100
[2]**vehicles** (n) things such as cars or buses which take people from one place to another, especially using roads

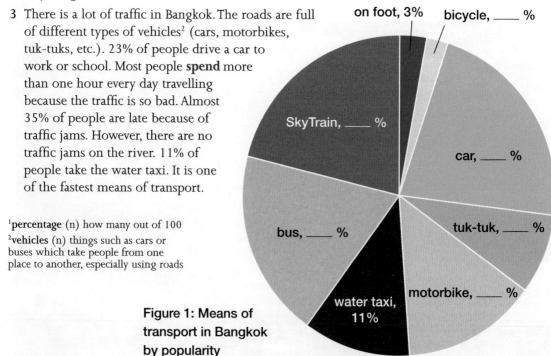

Figure 1: Means of transport in Bangkok by popularity

on foot, 3%   bicycle, ____ %
SkyTrain, ____ %
car, ____ %
bus, ____ %
tuk-tuk, ____ %
water taxi, 11%
motorbike, ____ %

5 Write the words and phrases from the box in the gaps. You can use a
word more than once. You may have to change verb form.

> drive   motorbikes   take   traffic   transport

> This report shows the results of a survey about (1)_____ in
> Bangkok. Over 8 million people live in Bangkok. The pie chart
> (Figure 1) shows the most popular types of transport in Bangkok.
> It shows the percentage of people who use each type of transport
> to get to work or school. 21% of the population of Bangkok
> (2)_____ the SkyTrain to work or school. Another way to
> travel is to (3)_____ the bus. However, it is more popular
> to (4)_____ your own car. There is a lot of (5)_____ in
> Bangkok. The roads are full of cars, (6)_____ , etc.

6 Read the text on page 178 again. Underline the information which answers
each question and write it below.

1 How many people live in Bangkok?

_____

2 Is the SkyTrain a public or private form of transport?

_____

3 What percentage of people drive cars?

_____

4 How long do most people spend in traffic?

_____

5 What percentage of people are late because of traffic jams?

_____

DISCUSSION

7 Ask and answer the questions with a partner.

1 What is the most popular way to get to work in Bangkok? Why do you
   think people prefer that type of transport?
2 Imagine you live in Bangkok. What type of transport would you use?
   Why?
3 Use information from Reading 1 and Reading 2 to answer the questions:
   Why is it important for cities to know how people get to work?
   Which type of transport do you think is best for cities? Why?

SUPERLATIVE ADJECTIVES

Superlative adjectives show how a noun in a group is different from all the other nouns. Superlative adjectives have different forms. Use *the* before a superlative adjective.

For one-syllable adjectives, add *-est*.	long ➞ the long**est** **The longest** trip is an hour.
For adjectives that end in one vowel + one consonant, double the consonant and add *-est*.	big ➞ the bi**ggest** The underground has **the biggest** station.
For adjectives that end in a consonant + *-y*, change the *-y* to *-i* and add *-est*.	dry ➞ the dr**iest** January is usually **the driest** month in Bangkok. friendly ➞ the friend**liest** Bangkok has **the friendliest** people.
For adjectives with two or more syllables, add *the most* before the adjective.	popular ➞ **the most** popular The SkyTrain is **the most popular** type of transport.
Some adjectives have irregular superlative forms.	good ➞ **the best** The water taxi is **the best** way to travel. bad ➞ **the worst** Driving is **the worst** way to travel here. There is always bad traffic.

1 Write the superlative form to replace the words in bold.

1 The tuk-tuks are **slow**. _____the slowest_____
2 My morning journey to work is **long**. _____
3 Bangkok has **hot** summers. _____
4 The roads are **busy**. _____
5 The centre is **an important** part of the city. _____
6 My journey to school is **short**. _____
7 The traffic is very **bad** in the morning. _____
8 The views are **pretty** from the water taxi. _____
9 The metro is **a good** way to travel. _____
10 The motorway is **a big** road in the city. _____

QUANTIFIERS

GRAMMAR

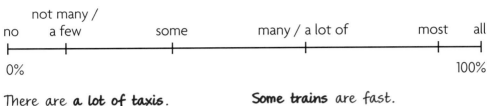

Quantifiers tell you the answer to the question *How many?* Use quantifiers before a noun. For small numbers, use *a few*, *not many* and *some*. For bigger numbers, use *many*, *a lot of* and *most*.

```
        not many /
no       a few            some          many / a lot of          most    all
├─────────┼──────────────────┼───────────────────┼──────────────────┼───────┤
0%                                                                      100%
```

There are **a lot of taxis**.   **Some trains** are fast.
A few people take tuk-tuks.   **Many people** work in the centre.
Not many people take taxis.   **Most people** drive their own cars.

2 Read the sentences. Circle the quantifiers and underline the nouns the quantifiers refer to.

1 Most people in Bangkok drive their own cars.
2 Some people ride motorbikes.
3 Not many people cycle to work or school.
4 A few people take the water taxi.
5 Many people take the SkyTrain.
6 Not many people walk to work or school.
7 Most people spend more than one hour travelling to work or school.

PLUS

3 Read the sentences and write quantifiers in the gaps. Use the percentages to help you. More than one answer is possible.

1 _____ (90%) people take the underground to work.
2 _____ (8%) people drive their cars to work.
3 _____ (25%) people cycle to work.
4 _____ (9%) people take the bus to work.
5 _____ (3%) people walk or run to work.
6 _____ (70%) students take the bus to the university.
7 _____ (0%) students drive to the university.
8 _____ (100%) employees work in the office.

TRANSPORT COLLOCATIONS

You can use these types of collocations when you talk about transport.

subject	verb	determiner	noun (transport)	prepositional phrase (*to* + place)
Many people	take	the	bus metro	to school. to work.
My parents	drive	their a	car	to work.
I	ride	my a	bike motorbike	to school.

subject	verb	prepositional phrase (*to* + place)	prepositional phrase (*by* + noun for transport)
Many students People	travel get	to school to work	by bus. by metro. by car.

4 Put the words in order to make sentences.

1 to / take / school / We / a bus / .

_____

2 travels / by / work / train / Malai / to / .

_____

3 takes / to / the city / the metro / Sunan / .

_____

4 get to / work / Many people / motorbike / by / .

_____

5 by / My children / bike / get to / school / .

_____

6 a taxi / to / the shop / Suni / takes / .

_____

5 Read the sentences. Write the correct form of the verbs in the gaps. You can use the words more than once.

> drive   ride   take

1 James _____ a motorbike. His mother does not like it.
2 I _____ a taxi to the airport.
3 Ali can _____ a bike to work.
4 Alison usually _____ the bus to school.
5 Keiko always _____ a car.

WRITING

CRITICAL THINKING

At the end of this unit, you are going to write about the results of a survey. Look at this unit's writing task in the box below.

> Write a paragraph explaining the results of a survey about transport.

Collecting and analyzing data

Before you write, you can *collect data* and *analyze* it. You can use questionnaires and surveys to collect data. Then look at it carefully. What does the data show? What can you do with this information?

1 Look back at Reading 2 on page 178. Tick (✔) the number of the paragraph or paragraphs that state the percentages in the pie chart.

_____ 1 _____ 2 _____ 3

UNDERSTAND

2 Now look at the results from a survey on transport in Chicago. Match the questions (1–3) to the results (a–c).

ANALYZE

We asked over one million workers the following questions:

1 Do you use public transport? If so, what type? _____
2 If you don't use public transport, how do you get to work? _____
3 Which statements do you agree with? _____

a The bus takes too long. There is too much traffic. The water taxi is not near my work. It takes too long to walk to my workplace.
b 17% take the train. 8% take the bus. 2% take a water taxi.
c 1% cycle to work. 7% walk to work. 3% take a taxi to work. The other 62% drive to work.

3 Underline the information in Exercise 2 that you could show in a pie chart.

4 Use the information from Exercise 2. Write the percentages in the pie chart.

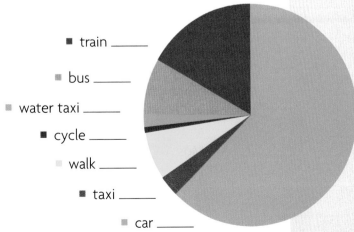

- train _____
- bus _____
- water taxi _____
- cycle _____
- walk _____
- taxi _____
- car _____

5 With a partner, ask and answer questions about the pie chart. Look at the percentages and how big or small each piece of the pie chart is.

    1 How do most workers in Chicago get to work?

    2 How do some workers in Chicago get to work?

    3 How do a few workers in Chicago get to work?

6 Discuss the results. Why do you think people use the different types of transport?

GRAMMAR FOR WRITING

SUBJECT–VERB–OBJECT

A sentence is about a *subject*. The subject is a *pronoun*, a *noun* or a *noun phrase*. The *verb* is after the subject in a sentence. A sentence can have an *object*. The object is a pronoun, a noun or a noun phrase. The object is after the verb.

subject: **14% of people** ride motorbikes.

11% of people take the water taxi.

verb: 14% of people **ride** motorbikes.

11% of people **take** the water taxi.

object of verb: 14% of people ride **motorbikes**.

11% of people take **the water taxi**.

A prepositional phrase is <u>not</u> the object of a verb.

                            prepositional phrase   *prepositional phrase*

Many students in the class travel **to school**   **by metro.**

                            prepositional phrase   *prepositional phrase*

A few students in the class get **to school**   **by car.**

1 Read the sentences. Tick (✔) if the bold word or phrase is the object of the verb.

    _____ 1 Many people travel **by car**.

    _____ 2 Many people in Hong Kong take **a water taxi** to work.

    _____ 3 Students in Rio de Janeiro do not cycle to their **universities**.

    _____ 4 In Costa Rica, families often ride **motorbikes** to work and school.

    _____ 5 Most people in Moscow travel **by metro**.

2 Read the sentences. Three of the sentences have objects. Find the objects and underline them.

1 Jamila and Kamilah travel to school by car.
2 Juan drives a car to university.
3 Some people walk to work in New York.
4 Many people ride bikes to work in London.
5 People in Bangkok often take the SkyTrain.

3 Work with a partner. Correct the mistakes in the sentences.

1 In Abu Dhabi, cars people drive to work.
_____

2 Not many people in Ankara take to work taxis.
_____

3 Workers in Seoul take the train work.
_____

4 Most students to school motorbikes ride.
_____

5 Some students in Paris take to university the bus.
_____

LINKING SENTENCES WITH PRONOUNS

GRAMMAR

Use *pronouns* when you do not want to repeat the same noun or noun phrase in a paragraph. The pronouns *he, she, it* and *they* can replace nouns. The nouns you replace can be *subjects* or *objects* in different sentences.

subject: **The pie chart** shows the most popular types of transport in Bangkok. ~~The pie chart~~ **It** shows the percentage of people who use each type of transport to get to work or school.

object: Many students ride **motorbikes**. ~~Motorbikes~~ **They** are not expensive.

4 Match the sentences (1–5) with (a–e). Use the correct pronouns. Make sure the bold words in a-e can replace the ones in 1–5.

1 **Jamila and Kamilah** travel to school by car. _____
2 **Jordan** drives a car to university. _____
3 **Some people** cycle to work in New York. _____
4 Many workers ride a **bike** to work in London. _____
5 People in Bangkok prefer to take the **SkyTrain**. _____

a **He** is a good driver.
b **It** is cheaper than a tuk-tuk!
c **It** is a healthy form of transport.
d **They** travel in their father's car.
e **They** can ride on special roads for bikes.

5 Read the pairs of sentences. Write the correct pronouns in the gaps.

1 Not many workers travel by **taxi**. _____ is an expensive type of transport.
2 Maria takes the **bus** to work. _____ does not drive.
3 **Students** in Mexico City do not cycle to university. _____ drive there.
4 In Chile, **families** often drive a car to work and school. _____ travel together.
5 Most people in Tokyo travel by **metro**. _____ is the busiest metro system in the world.

ACADEMIC WRITING SKILLS

GIVING REASONS WITH *BECAUSE* AND RESULTS WITH *SO*

Use *because* and *so* to show reasons and results. Sentences with *because* and *so* often have two clauses which each have a subject and a verb. The clause after *because* is the reason clause.

subject   verb   *subject   verb*
People prefer buses to tuk-tuks **because** buses cost less money.

The clause after *so* is the *result* clause. Put a comma before *so* to show a result.

subject   verb   *subject   verb*
Saad takes public transport, **so** he leaves his car at home.

Use *because of* to give a reason before pronouns, nouns or noun phrases.

                                                               noun phrase
Almost 35% of people are late **because of** traffic jams.

1 Match the sentence halves.

1 Most people spend more than one hour every day travelling _____
2 Many people travel by water taxi _____
3 Many people cycle to work, _____
4 Taxis are expensive, _____
5 People don't ride motorbikes _____

a so not many people take them.
b because the traffic is so bad.
c so the city now has special roads for bikes.
d because of rain.
e because the city is on a river.

2 Complete each sentence. Use your own ideas to give reasons or results. Then share your sentences with a partner.

1 In my city, only a few people walk to work _____
   _____ .

2 Many people take the bus or train to school _____
   _____ .

3 A few people take taxis to work _____
   _____ .

4 Driving a car takes a long time _____
   _____ .

WRITING TASK

Write a paragraph explaining the results of a survey about transport.

PLAN

1 Look at the results of the survey and pie chart from the Critical thinking section on page 183. What are the most popular and least popular types of transport?

2 You are going to use the results to write about transport in Chicago. Read the Task checklist on page 188 as you prepare your paragraph.

WRITE A FIRST DRAFT

3 Write your topic sentence first. See Unit 4 for help with paragraph structure.

4 Write sentences to add details about the topic.

1 Write a sentence about the seven forms of transport in the survey.
2 Write three or four sentences about the percentage of people who use each form of transport.
3 Write two or three sentences which compare popular forms of transport in the city.
4 Write two sentences which give reasons why people use the different types of transport.
5 Write a sentence about the most popular form of transport in the city.
6 Write a concluding sentence.

5 Put your topic sentence, supporting sentences and concluding sentence together to make a paragraph.

EDIT

6 Use the Task checklist to review your paragraph.

TASK CHECKLIST	✔
Use data from the survey on transport in Chicago.	
Use percentages from your pie chart.	
Write a topic sentence, supporting sentences and a concluding sentence.	
Use pronoun links in your sentences.	
Use *because* and *so* to give reasons and results.	
Use the correct form of superlative adjectives.	

7 Make any necessary changes to your paragraph.

OBJECTIVES REVIEW

1 Check your learning objectives for this unit. Write *3, 2* or *1* for each objective.

   3 = very well   2 = well   1 = not so well

   I can ...

   watch and understand a video about metros. ———

   work out meaning from context. ———

   collect and analyze data. ———

   use superlative adjectives. ———

   use quantifiers. ———

   use subject–verb–object sentence order. ———

   link sentences with pronouns. ———

   give reasons with *because* and results with *so*. ———

   write a paragraph explaining the results of a survey. ———

2 Go to the *Unlock* Online Workbook for more practice with this unit's learning objectives.

WORDLIST		
bicycle (n)	prefer (v) ⊙	take (v) ⊙
bus (n)	report (n) ⊙	taxi (n)
drive (v) ⊙	result (n) ⊙	traffic (n) ⊙
metro (n)	ride (v)	train (n) ⊙
motorbike (n)	spend (v) ⊙	transport (n) ⊙

⊙ = high-frequency words in the Cambridge Academic Corpus

GLOSSARY

⊙ = high-frequency words in the Cambridge Academic Corpus

Vocabulary	Pronunciation	Part of speech	Definition
UNIT 1			
aunt	/ɑːnt/	(n)	the sister of someone's mother or father, or the wife of someone's uncle
brother ⊙	/ˈbrʌðə/	(n)	a boy or man who has the same parents as you
city ⊙	/ˈsɪti/	(n)	a large town
country ⊙	/ˈkʌntri/	(n)	an area of land which has its own government, army, etc.
date of birth	/ˈdeɪt əv bɜːθ/	(n)	the day you were born, shown in numbers, or words and numbers
daughter ⊙	/ˈdɔːtə/	(n)	someone's female child
family ⊙	/ˈfæməli/	(n)	a group of people related to each other, such as a mother, a father and their children
father	/ˈfɑːðə/	(n)	someone's male parent
grandfather	/ˈgrænd,fɑːðə/	(n)	the father of someone's mother or father
grandmother	/ˈgrænd,mʌðə/	(n)	the mother of someone's mother or father
hobby	/ˈhɒbi/	(n)	an activity that you like and often do when you are not working
interested in	/ˈɪntrəstɪd ɪn/	(adj phr)	wanting to learn more about something

Vocabulary	Pronunciation	Part of speech	Definition
job ⊙	/dʒɒb/	(n)	the work which you do in order to get money
language ⊙	/ˈlæŋgwɪdʒ/	(n)	the words used by the people of a country
live ⊙	/lɪv/	(v)	to have your home somewhere
mother ⊙	/ˈmʌðə/	(n)	someone's female parent
music ⊙	/ˈmjuːzɪk/	(n)	sounds that are made by playing instruments or singing
normal ⊙	/ˈnɔːməl/	(adj)	usual, ordinary and expected
sister ⊙	/ˈsɪstə/	(n)	a girl or woman who has the same parents as you
son ⊙	/sʌn/	(n)	someone's male child
uncle	/ˈʌŋkl/	(n)	the brother of someone's mother or father, or the husband of someone's aunt
unusual ⊙	/ʌnˈjuːʒuəl/	(adj)	different and not usual, often in a way which is interesting or exciting
watch ⊙	/wɒtʃ/	(v)	to look at something for some time
work ⊙	/wɜːk/	(v)	to do a job, especially the job you do to get money

UNIT 2

Vocabulary	Pronunciation	Part of speech	Definition
autumn ⊙	/ɔːtəm/	(n)	the season of the year between summer and winter
climate ⊙	/klaɪmət/	(n)	the weather that a place usually has
cloudy	/klaʊdi/	(adj)	with many clouds in the sky

Vocabulary	Pronunciation	Part of speech	Definition
cold ⊙	/kəʊld/	(adj)	having a low temperature
dry ⊙	/draɪ/	(adj)	with very little or no rain
rainfall ⊙	/ˈreɪnfɔːl/	(n)	the amount of rain that falls in one place
rainy	/ˈreɪni/	(adj)	raining a lot
season ⊙	/ˈsiːzən/	(n)	one of the four periods of the year: winter, spring, summer or autumn
spring ⊙	/sprɪŋ/	(n)	the season of the year between winter and summer
summer ⊙	/ˈsʌmə/	(n)	the warmest season of the year, between spring and autumn
sunny	/sʌni/	(adj)	bright because of light from the sun
warm ⊙	/wɔːm/	(adj)	having a temperature between cool and hot
windy ⊙	/wɪndi/	(adj)	with a lot of wind
winter	/ˈwɪntə/	(n)	the coldest season of the year, between autumn and spring

UNIT 3

afternoon	/ˌɑːftəˈnuːn/	(n)	the time between 12 pm and 6 pm
Arabic	/ˈærəbɪk/	(n)	a language spoken in Western Asia and North Africa
Art ⊙	/ɑːt/	(n)	the making or study of paintings, drawings, etc. or the objects created
Biology ⊙	/baɪˈɒlədʒi/	(n)	the study of living things

Vocabulary	Pronunciation	Part of speech	Definition
breakfast	/ˈbrekfəst/	(n)	the food you eat in the morning after you wake up
Business ⊙	/ˈbɪznɪs/	(n)	the buying and selling of goods or services
busy ⊙	/ˈbɪzi/	(adj)	having a lot of things to do
Chemistry ⊙	/ˈkemɪstri/	(n)	the scientific study of substances and how they change when they combine
cook ⊙	/kʊk/	(v)	to prepare food by heating it
dinner	/ˈdɪnə/	(n)	the food you eat at the end of the day
Economics ⊙	/ˌiːkəˈnɒmɪks/	(n)	the study of the way in which trade, industry and money are organized
English ⊙	/ˈɪŋglɪʃ/	(n)	the language that is spoken in the UK, the US and in many other countries
evening ⊙	/ˈiːvnɪŋ/	(n)	the time between 6 pm and 11 pm
Geography	/dʒiˈɒgrəfi/	(n)	the study of the systems and processes involved in the world's weather, mountains, seas, lakes, etc.
get up	/get ʌp/	(phr v)	to leave your bed after sleeping
History ⊙	/ˈhɪstəri/	(n)	the study of events in the past
Literature	/ˈlɪtrətʃər/	(n)	written artistic works, especially those with a high and lasting artistic value
lunch	/lʌntʃ/	(n)	the food you eat in the middle of the day

Vocabulary	Pronunciation	Part of speech	Definition
Management	/'mænɪdʒmənt/	(n)	the study of the technique, practice or science of managing a company, business, etc.
Maths	/mæθs/	(n)	the study or science of numbers and shapes
meet ⊙	/miːt/	(v)	to see and speak to someone for the first time
morning ⊙	/'mɔːnɪŋ/	(n)	the time between 5 am and 12 pm
Physics ⊙	/'fɪzɪks/	(n)	the scientific study of natural forces, such as energy, heat, light, etc.
relax	/rɪ'læks/	(v)	to become calm and comfortable
Science ⊙	/saɪəns/	(n)	the study of the structure of natural things and the way that they behave
swim	/swɪm/	(v)	to move through water by moving your body
timetable	/'taɪmˌteɪbl/	(n)	a list or plan to show when you do things
travel ⊙	/'trævəl/	(v)	to go from one place to another, usually over a long distance
weekdays	/'wiːkdeɪz/	(n)	the five days of the week when many people work
weekend	/ˌwiːk'end/	(n)	the two days of the week when many people do not work

Vocabulary	Pronunciation	Part of speech	Definition
UNIT 4			
beach	/biːtʃ/	(n)	an area of sand or rocks next to a sea, ocean or lake
capital ⊙	/ˈkæpɪtəl/	(n)	the most important city in a country, where the government is
cliff	/klɪf/	(n)	a high area of rock with a very steep side, often next to a coast
desert ⊙	/ˈdezət/	(n)	a large, hot, dry area of land with very few plants
famous ⊙	/ˈfeɪməs/	(adj)	many people know it
farm ⊙	/fɑːm/	(n)	land and buildings used for growing crops and keeping animals
field ⊙	/ˈfiːld/	(n)	an area of land used for growing crops or keeping animals
forest ⊙	/ˈfɒrɪst/	(n)	a large area of trees growing closely together
hill ⊙	/hɪl/	(n)	a high area of land that is smaller than a mountain
international ⊙	/ˌɪntəˈnæʃənəl/	(adj)	relating to or involving two or more countries
island ⊙	/ˈaɪlənd/	(n)	land with water all around it
lake ⊙	/leɪk/	(n)	an area of fresh water which has land all around it
map ⊙	/mæp/	(n)	a picture which shows a place and the rivers, lakes and other areas in it
modern ⊙	/ˈmɒdən/	(adj)	made with new ideas and designs

Vocabulary	Pronunciation	Part of speech	Definition
mountain ⊙	/'maʊntɪn/	(n)	a very high hill
ocean ⊙	/'əʊʃən/	(n)	one of the five main areas of salt water on the Earth
popular ⊙	/'pɒpjələ/	(adj)	many people like it
river ⊙	/'rɪvə/	(n)	water which flows across the land to a bigger area of water
sea ⊙	/siː/	(n)	a large area of salt water
tourist	/'tʊərɪst/	(n)	a person who travels and visits places for fun
valley ⊙	/'væli/	(n)	an area of low land between hills or mountains

UNIT 5

Vocabulary	Pronunciation	Part of speech	Definition
company ⊙	/'kʌmpəni/	(n)	an organization which sells something to make money
doctor ⊙	/'dɒktə/	(n)	a person with a medical degree whose job is to treat people who are ill or hurt
engineer ⊙	/ˌendʒɪ'nɪə/	(n)	a person who designs and builds things
farmer ⊙	/'fɑːmə/	(n)	someone who owns or looks after a farm
fit ⊙	/fɪt/	(adj)	in good health; strong
fitness instructor	/'fɪtnəs ɪn'strʌktə/	(n)	somebody who teaches people how to do exercises
football player	/'fʊtbɔːl 'pleɪə/	(n)	someone who plays football, especially as their job
friendly ⊙	/'frendli/	(adj)	nice and kind
good at	/gʊd ət/	(adj)	able to do something well

Vocabulary	Pronunciation	Part of speech	Definition
great ◉	/greɪt/	(adj)	very good; excellent
gym	/dʒɪm/	(n)	a place with machines where people go to do exercises
healthy ◉	/ˈhelθi/	(adj)	being well; not sick
high school	/ˈhaɪ ˌskuːl/	(n)	a school for children from about 12 to 18 years old
hospital ◉	/ˈhɒspɪtəl/	(n)	a place where people who are sick or hurt go for help
interesting ◉	/ˈɪntrəstɪŋ/	(adj)	exciting; not boring
journalist	/ˈdʒɜːnəlɪst/	(n)	a person who writes news stories or articles for a newspaper or magazine or broadcasts them on radio or television
language teacher	/ˈlæŋgwɪdʒ ˈtiːtʃə/	(n)	somebody who teaches languages
manager ◉	/ˈmænɪdʒə/	(n)	a person who is responsible for managing an organization
medicine ◉	/ˈmedɪsən/	(n)	something you take to feel better
nurse ◉	/nɜːs/	(n)	a person who helps doctors and cares for people
office ◉	/ˈɒfɪs/	(n)	a room or part of a building in which people work
pay ◉	/peɪ/	(n)	the money you receive for doing a job
pilot ◉	/ˈpaɪlət/	(n)	a person who flies an aeroplane
school ◉	/skuːl/	(n)	a place where children go to be educated

Vocabulary	Pronunciation	Part of speech	Definition
school teacher	/ˈskuːl ˈtiːtʃə/	(n)	somebody who teaches children at a school
software engineer	/ˈsɒftweər ˌendʒɪˈnɪə/	(n)	someone whose job is to create computer programs

UNIT 6

Vocabulary	Pronunciation	Part of speech	Definition
apartment	/əˈpɑːtmənt/	(n)	a set of rooms for someone to live in on one level of a building or house
beautiful ⊙	/ˈbjuːtɪfəl/	(adj)	very attractive
big ⊙	/bɪg/	(adj)	large in size or amount
building	/ˈbɪldɪŋ/	(n)	a structure with walls and a roof, such as a house, school, etc.
car park	/ˈkɑː ˌpɑːk/	(n)	a place where vehicles can be parked
ceiling	/ˈsiːlɪŋ/	(n)	the surface of a room that you can see when you look above you
cheap ⊙	/tʃiːp/	(adj)	costing little money
cost ⊙	/kɒst/	(v)	to have an amount of money as a price; you must pay that amount to buy something
entrance ⊙	/ˈentrəns/	(n)	a door or other opening that you use to enter a building or place
exit ⊙	/ˈeksɪt/	(n)	the door or gate that you use to leave a building or place
expensive ⊙	/ɪkˈspensɪv/	(adj)	costing a lot of money
garden ⊙	/ˈgɑːdən/	(n)	an area of ground belonging to a house, often containing grass, flowers or trees

Vocabulary	Pronunciation	Part of speech	Definition
glass ⊙	/glɑːs/	(n)	a hard, transparent material, used to make windows, bottles and other objects
lift ⊙	/lɪft/	(n)	a machine which carries people up and down in tall buildings
modern ⊙	/ˈmɒdən/	(adj)	relating to the present and not the past; using the newest ideas, design, technology, etc.
new ⊙	/njuː/	(adj)	different from before; recently made
old ⊙	/əʊld/	(adj)	having lived or existed for a long time; having been used or owned for a long time
plastic ⊙	/ˈplæstɪk/	(adj)	made of a light, artificial substance which can be made into different shapes when it is soft and is used in a lot of different ways
roof ⊙	/ruːf/	(n)	the surface which covers the top of a building or vehicle
shopping centre	/ˈʃɒpɪŋ ˌsentə/	(n)	a place where a lot of shops have been built close together
short ⊙	/ʃɔːt/	(adj)	having a small distance from one end to the other
small ⊙	/smɔːl/	(adj)	little in size or amount
stairs ⊙	/steəz/	(n)	a set of steps from one level in a building to another
tall ⊙	/tɔːl/	(adj)	having a greater than average height
traditional ⊙	/trəˈdɪʃənəl/	(adj)	following the customs or ways of behaving which have continued in a group of people or society for a long time

Vocabulary	Pronunciation	Part of speech	Definition
ugly ⊙	/ˈʌgli/	(adj)	unpleasant to look at
wall ⊙	/wɔːl/	(n)	one of the vertical sides of a room or building
window ⊙	/ˈwɪndəʊ/	(n)	a space in the wall of a building or in a vehicle which has glass in it, used for letting light and air inside and for looking through
wood ⊙	/wʊd/	(n)	the hard material which trees are made of

UNIT 7

Vocabulary	Pronunciation	Part of speech	Definition
almond	/ˈɑːmənd/	(n)	a flat, oval nut, often used in cooking
bread ⊙	/bred/	(n)	a basic food made from flour, water and salt mixed together and baked
chilli	/ˈtʃɪli/	(n)	a small, thin, red or green vegetable which tastes very hot
coconut	/ˈkəʊkənʌt/	(n)	a very large nut with a hard, hairy shell, a white part which you eat and liquid in the centre
date ⊙	/deɪt/	(n)	a sticky brown fruit with a long seed inside
different ⊙	/ˈdɪfərənt/	(adj)	not like other things
dish	/dɪʃ/	(n)	food that is prepared in a particular way as part of a meal
drink	/drɪŋk/	(n)	a liquid that you can put in your mouth and swallow, like water or juice
fish ⊙	/fɪʃ/	(n)	an animal which lives in water and swims using its tail and fins, eaten as food

Vocabulary	Pronunciation	Part of speech	Definition
honey	/ˈhʌni/	(n)	a sweet and sticky food made by bees
jam	/dʒæm/	(n)	a sweet food made from fruit which you spread on bread
meal ⊙	/mɪəl/	(n)	the food which is eaten at a particular time or for a particular event
meat ⊙	/miːt/	(n)	muscles and the soft parts of animals, used as food
milk	/mɪlk/	(n)	a white liquid produced by women and other female animals, such as cows, for feeding their babies
onion	/ˈʌnjən/	(n)	a round vegetable with layers which has a strong taste and smell
prepare ⊙	/prɪˈpeə/	(v)	to make something
rice	/raɪs/	(n)	small grains from a plant which are cooked and eaten as food
same	/seɪm/	(adj)	like something else
serve with	/sɜːv wɪð/	(v phr)	to give someone food with other food on the same plate or as part of the same meal
spice	/spaɪs/	(n)	a substance made from a plant, used to give a special taste to food
type	/taɪp/	(n)	something which is part of a group of things which are like each other
vegetable	/ˈvedʒtəbəl/	(n)	a plant which you eat, for example, potato, onion, bean, etc.

Vocabulary	Pronunciation	Part of speech	Definition
water	/ˈwɔːtə/	(n)	a clear liquid which falls from the sky as rain and which is in seas, lakes and rivers
yoghurt	/ˈjɒgət/	(n)	a thick, liquid food with a slightly sour taste which is made from milk

UNIT 8

Vocabulary	Pronunciation	Part of speech	Definition
bicycle	/ˈbaɪsɪkl/	(n)	a type of transport with two wheels that you sit on and move by pushing two pedals with your feet
bus	/bʌs/	(n)	a big type of car which carries many passengers by road
drive ⊙	/draɪv/	(v)	to make a car, bus or train move, and control what it does
metro	/ˈmetrəʊ/	(n)	trains which travel underground, usually in a city
motorbike	/ˈməʊtəbaɪk/	(n)	a type of transport with two wheels and an engine
prefer ⊙	/prɪˈfɜː/	(v)	to like someone or something more than another person or thing
report ⊙	/rɪˈpɔːt/	(n)	information about an event or situation
result ⊙	/rɪˈzʌlt/	(n)	information which you get from something, like an exam, a survey, a medical test, etc.
ride	/raɪd/	(v)	to travel by sitting on a bicycle or motorbike, in a bus or metro, etc.

Vocabulary	Pronunciation	Part of speech	Definition
spend ◉	/spend/	(v)	to use time by doing something
take ◉	/teɪk/	(v)	to travel somewhere using a taxi, bus or train
taxi	/'tæksi/	(n)	a car with a driver who you pay to take you somewhere
traffic ◉	/'træfɪk/	(n)	the cars, trucks, etc. driving on the road
train ◉	/treɪn/	(n)	a long, thin type of transport which travels on metal tracks and carries people or things
transport ◉	/'trænspɔːt/	(n)	the things people use to move themselves or things from one place to another

UNIT 1

▶ Fishermen

Narrator: Fish is a part of a healthy diet. And people all over the world are eating more and more of it – about 20 kilograms per person per year. That's more than 100,000 tonnes of fish. We can thank the more than 57 million people who work as fishermen for all that fish. They go out every day in 4.6 million boats. Most of them are small boats, like these boats on the coast of India. Fourteen million people in India are fishermen. They catch fish to feed their families and to sell. These fishermen use nets to catch fish.

Most of those 57 million fishermen are in Asia and Africa, but there are also plenty of fishermen in Europe, like this man. He fishes from a boat near the coast of England. Some of this man's catch may end up like this, in fish and chips – a popular dish in the United Kingdom, where people spend 1.2 billion pounds every year in the country's more than 10,000 fish and chip shops! Almost a quarter of the British population visits a fish and chip shop every week.

For most fishermen, fishing is a job. But for others, it's a way to relax. Many of these people bring their fishing rods to the Galata Bridge in Istanbul, in Turkey, every day. Sometimes they catch a big fish, sometimes it's just a little one, but they can always enjoy some tea and time with their friends.

UNIT 2

▶ The taiga forest

Narrator: In the beginning of winter here, the days grow short and cold. Snow and cold temperatures move south into parts of North America, Europe and Asia.

Winter is hard here. Water in the air, in rivers and in plants turns to ice. As a result, most of the plants die. But some trees, like fir trees and pine trees, can live in very cold temperatures. These trees make up the greatest forest on Earth, called the taiga.

The taiga forest goes around the northern part of the Earth. From Alaska to Canada, from Scandinavia to Russia, it has almost 30% of all the trees on Earth!

During the winter, in the most northern part of the taiga forest, freezing air from the north meets warm air from the south. Heavy snow covers this area of the taiga until warmer temperatures return in the spring.

UNIT 3

▶ Toronto tourism

Narrator: Toronto, Canada, sits on the northern shore of Lake Ontario. With 2.8 million people, it's the country's largest city. It's also a fun place to visit. Forty million tourists visit Toronto every year. It has many tourist attractions, like this one. Over a million people visit this square each year to listen to concerts, go ice skating or just shop.

But Toronto's most famous attraction is the CN Tower. The tower opened in 1976 and very quickly became popular with visitors, but its main purpose is for communication. At 553 metres tall, it's the tallest building in the city. Visitors can take a tram to the tower. You can see the main pod about halfway up the tower. That's where most visitors go.

The LookOut level in the main pod is 346 metres above ground. From here, you can have a 360-degree view of the city and the lake. On the same level, you can also visit the Glass Floor. When you walk out onto the floor, you can look straight down through the glass to the ground.

If you want to go even higher, visit the SkyPod. It is 447 metres above the ground. From the SkyPod, on a clear day, you can see for 160 kilometres – all the way to Niagara Falls, near the Canadian-United States border. Of course Niagara Falls looks much smaller from the CN Tower!

If you are very brave, you may want to try the EdgeWalk. You and five friends can walk around the outside of the main pod. When you look down, there is nothing between you and the city of Toronto, 116 floors below!

UNIT 4

▶ The *cenotes* of Mexico

Narrator: In the southeast part of Mexico, known as the Yucatán, there are many rich, green forests.

Here, these amazing holes are the only spaces in the trees. They are very deep, they are made of rock and they are often full of water. Mexicans call these places *cenotes*.

Olmo Torres-Talamante is a scientist. For him, the *cenotes* are very special. He studies them, and the plants and animals in and around them.

Water is very important in the Yucatán. It rains a lot here, but there are no lakes or rivers. When it rains, the water goes down into the rock under the Yucatán. Over time, it makes the *cenotes*.

Cenotes are the only places to find fresh water in the Yucatán. They help the animals and plants in the forest live.

Lily pads, fish and turtles all live at the top of the *cenotes*, where it's warm and light.

But when Olmo swims deeper into the cave, it gets cold and dark. How can anything live here?

But even here, the scientist finds life.

UNIT 5

▶ Utah's Bingham mine

Narrator: This is the Bingham copper mine in Utah, in the western United States. It's the largest mine of its kind in the world. And it gets bigger all the time. Today it's two and a half miles wide and almost one mile deep.

Matt Lengerich is the operations manager of the mine. It produces enough copper each year to make wires for every home in the USA and Mexico. We use copper everywhere – in our homes, cell phones and cars – and some of it comes from here.

But the rocks contain only a small amount of copper. So Matt's workers have to dig up a lot of rocks to get enough copper. That's why Bingham mine is so big.

Matt's workers use these giant trucks to dig up the copper. Sometimes the copper is so deep that they have to dig for seven years to reach it.

Everything about the mine is big. These giant trucks are heavier than a jumbo jet and work 24 hours a day.

Drivers use the giant trucks to move the rocks and copper. But they also use something stronger.

The Bingham mine is more than 100 years old and it's larger than any other mine of its kind.

UNIT 6

▶ Living in Singapore

Narrator: Singapore. It's an island, a city and a country. It's an important centre for banking, technology and transport. And it's growing. It has the second busiest port in the world. With an area of less than 720 square kilometres and five and a half million people, space is a problem. Where does everyone live?

In the first half of the 20th century, many people lived in buildings like these. There are shops on the bottom floor, and people live on the second floor. But there were not enough houses or flats for the growing population. The government began to build hundreds of tall apartment buildings like these. The apartments are modern, simple and light. Today more than 80% of the population lives in these buildings. Groups of buildings create high-rise neighbourhoods, with schools, shopping, restaurants and medical offices nearby.

About 10% of all tourists arrive by cruise ship, and there are lots of hotels. The country has more than a million hotel rooms for all of the tourists and business travellers. There are traditional hotels. This one is probably Singapore's most famous hotel – Raffles. It was built in 1887, when Singapore was part of the British Empire. Most hotels in the city are modern. This luxury hotel stands next to the sea.

But for the people of Singapore, this looks like home. More than 90% of them own their home – one of the highest rates in the world.

UNIT 7

▶ Goat's cheese

Narrator: This is the village of Arreau in the south of France. Every Thursday morning in Arreau, there is a market. Here, farmers sell fruit, vegetables, bread, meat and cheese.

Cheese is very popular in France. And Arreau has some very special cheese – goat cheese. Mrs Tuchan sells goat cheese from her farm. Her farm is in a village near Arreau. People can visit the farm to learn how she and her husband make cheese.

First they have to get the milk from the goats. The goats wait at the door. They go into the milking room one by one. Mrs Tuchan uses a machine to get the milk. She does this twice a day. Each goat can give more than two quarts of milk every day.

Next, the milk goes to a different room – the cheese-making room.

Now they have to turn the milk into cheese. Mr Tuchan adds an ingredient to the goat milk. Then he puts it in small plastic cups with holes in the bottom.

The next day, he turns the cheese over. Then he adds some salt to it.

Next, he moves the cheese to another room. The cheese stays here for one to three weeks. Then it will be ready to sell, and to eat.

UNIT 8

▶ Modern metros

Narrator: How do people in big cities travel? Many of them take the underground. Underground trains move millions of people underground every day. There are over 150 underground systems in the world today. The oldest one is in London, England. There, everyone calls it the 'Tube'.

At 8:00 am, the Tube really gets busy. In the morning, over 500,000 Londoners go to work by underground. Of course, people on the streets can't see them. But what if the Tube ran above the ground?

Every day in London, over 500 trains on 250 miles of track move nearly 3 million people. That's a lot of people, but the busiest underground system in the world is in Tokyo, Japan.

There are more people in Tokyo than in any other city in the world. Around 35,000 people take the Tokyo underground every hour. That means eight million passengers travel underground every day. On every platform, there are 25 underground attendants, like Yuhei Mitsuhashi. They keep the passengers safe, calm and on time, because the trains cannot be late.

The authors and publishers acknowledge the following sources of copyright material and are grateful for the permissions granted. While every effort has been made, it has not always been possible to identify the sources of all the material used, or to trace all copyright holders. If any omissions are brought to our notice, we will be happy to include the appropriate acknowledgements on reprinting and in the next update to the digital edition, as applicable.

Key: B = Below, C = Centre, BL = Below Left, BC = Below Centre, BR = Below Right, L = Left, R = Right, T = Top, TL = Top Left, TR = Top Right.

Photos
All below images are sourced from Getty Images.

pp. 14–15: Alexander Spatari/Moment; p. 19: Julian Herbert/Getty Images Sport; p. 22 (T): BERND THISSEN/DPA; p. 22 (B): Mac99/iStock/Getty Images Plus; p. 29 (T): Juanmonino/E+; p. 29 (B): Linghe Zhao/The Image Bank; pp. 36–37: Sean Pavone/iStock/Getty Images Plus; p. 41 (TL): noblige/iStock/Getty Images Plus; p. 41 (TR): wojciech_gajda/iStock/Getty Images Plus; p. 41 (B): Bill Bachmann/First Light; p. 44: Kriangkrai Thitimakorn/Moment; p. 52: Roy Cheung/Moment; p. 55: jeff1961/Multi-bits/The Image Bank; p. 55: jeff1961/Multi-bits/The Image Bank; pp. 58–59: Lonely Planet Images; p. 63 (T, BL): John Noble/Lonely Planet Images; p. 63 (BR): Johnny Haglund/Lonely Planet Images; pp. 80–81: John and Tina Reid/Moment; p. 84 (1): Bestgreenscreen/iStock/Getty Images Plus; p. 84 (2), p. 85: Universal Images Group; p. 84 (3): Maureen P Sullivan/Moment; p. 84 (4): Mike Kemp/In Pictures; p. 84 (5): Image Source; p. 84 (6): Chad Baker/DigitalVision; p. 84 (7), p. 94: Martin Barraud/Stone; p. 88 (R): Buena Vista Images/Photodisc; p. 99: David Crespo/Moment; pp. 102–103: Reza/Getty Images News; p. 110 (T): WIN-Initiative; p. 110 (C): JohnnyGreig/E+; p. 110 (B): Hill Street Studios/Blend Images; pp. 124–125: JaCZhou 2015/Moment Open; p. 128 (a): Matheisl/Photographer's Choice; p. 128 (b): kcconsulting/iStock/Getty Images Plus; p. 128 (c): Joho/Cultura; p. 128 (d): S.B. Nace/Lonely Planet Images; p. 128 (e): pbombaert/Moment; p. 128 (f): FUTURE LIGHT/Photolibrary; p. 128 (g): Peter Starman/Photographer's Choice RF; p. 128 (h): Zsolt Bute/EyeEm; p. 129 (T): Jetta Productions/Iconica; p. 129 (BL): View Pictures/Universal Images Group; p. 129 (BC): Deconphotostudio; p. 129 (BR): Architecture: Bureau LADA + Kettinghuls, Photographer: Thomas Landen; p. 132 (L): gionnixxx/iStock/Getty Images plus; p. 132 (C): Gavin Hellier/AWL Images; p. 132 (R): Ed Norton/Lonely Planet Images; p. 134: George Rose/Getty Images News; p. 141: Iain Masterton/arabianEye; p. 151: BJI/Blue Jean Images; p. 152 (T): Carlina Teteris/Moment; p. 152 (C): Danita Delimont/Gallo Images; p. 154 (a): Antonio Ciufo/Moment Open; p. 154 (b): James Smedley/First Light; p. 154 (c): Bridget Davey/Moment Mobile; p. 154 (d): Kelvin Kam/EyeEm; p. 154 (e): Jennifer Levy/StockFood Creative; p. 156 (T): Hisham Ibrahim/Moment Mobile; p. 156 (C): Amateur photographer, still learning/Moment Open; p. 156 (B): Martin Robinson/Lonely Planet Images; p. 157 (photo 2, photo 4, photo 6, photo 7, photo 8, photo 11): iStockphoto/Thinkstock; p. 157 (photo 3): Gregoria Gregoriou Crowe fine art and creative photography. Creative/Moment; p. 157 (photo 5): naruedom/iStock/Getty Images Plus; p. 157 (photo 10): Stockbyte/Thinkstock; p. 168–169: Thanapol Marattana/Moment; p. 173 (L): Will Gray/AWL Images; p. 173 (C): AaronChenPs/Moment; p. 173 (R): Joel Carillet/E+; p. 175: Dulyanut Swdp/Moment; p. 176: Universal Images Group.

The following images are from other image libraries:
p. 88 (L): Photogerson/Shutterstock; pp. 146–147: Steve Vidler/Alamy Stock Photo; p. 152 (B): Gaza Press/REX/Shutterstock; p. 157 (photo 1): © Iilya Akinshin/Shutterstock; p. 157 (photo 9): © Mariyana Misaleva/Shutterstock; p. 157 (photo 12): © Viktar Malyshchyts/Shutterstock.

Front cover photography by Barry Kusuma/Photolibrary.

Video stills
All below stills are sourced from Getty Images.

p. 16 (video 1, video 4): Sky News/Film Image Partner; p. 16 (video 2): Clippn/Getty Images Editorial Footage; p. 16 (video 3): Fuji Television Network, Inc./Image Bank Film; p. 60 (video 1, video 4): Faithfulshot – Footage/Getty Images Editorial Footage; p. 60 (video 2): OrlowskiDesigns/Creatas Video+/Getty Images Plus; p. 60 (video 3): Roberto Machado Noa/LightRocket; p. 126 (video 1): Charles Yeo/Creatas Video+/Getty Images Plus; p. 126 (video 2, video 4): AFP Footage; p. 126 (video 3): Discovery FootageSource.

The following stills are sourced from other libraries.

p. 38, p. 82, p. 104, p. 126, p. 148, p. 170: BBC Worldwide Learning.

Illustrations
p. 91: Rudolf Farkas; p. 88: Martin Sanders.

Videos
Videos supplied by BBC Worldwide Learning and Getty Images.

Sky News/Film Image Partner; NewsHour Productions – Footage/Getty Images Editorial Footage; Eastfootage/Image Bank Film; Fuji Television Network, Inc./Image Bank Film; AFP Footage/AFP; Clippn/Getty Images Editorial Footage; Willem Viljoen, Teneighty/Image Bank Film; Mark Kolbe/Getty Images Editorial Footage; Daniel Coolahan/Getty Images Editorial Footage; Cordell Jigsaw Productions/Image Bank Film; davidf/Creatas Video; ifolio/Creatas Video+/Getty Images Plus; Ariel Skelley/Image Bank Film; Faithfulshot – Footage/Getty Images Editorial Footage; BBC Motion Gallery Editorial/BBC News/BBC Editorial; am1tk/iStock/Getty Images Plus; ullstein bild; Vividus/Creatas Video+/Getty Images Plus; FatCamera/Creatas Video; Travel Productions/Image Bank Film; Chuck and Sarah Fishbein/Iconica Video; primeimages/Creatas Video; Dorian Weber/Verve; Charles Yeo/Creatas Video+/Getty Images Plus; Bloomberg Video – Footage/Bloomberg; catchlights_sg/Creatas Video; Pavel Gospodinov/Image Bank Film; Pierre Ogeron/Photodisc; BBC Worldwide Learning.

Corpus
Development of this publication has made use of the Cambridge English Corpus (CEC). The CEC is a multi-billion word computer database of contemporary spoken and written English. It includes British English, American English and other varieties of English. It also includes the Cambridge Learner Corpus, developed in collaboration with the University of Cambridge ESOL Examinations. Cambridge University Press has built up the CEC to provide evidence about language use that helps to produce better language teaching materials.

Cambridge Dictionaries
Cambridge dictionaries are the world's most widely used dictionaries for learners of English. The dictionaries are available in print and online at dictionary.cambridge.org. Copyright © Cambridge University Press, reproduced with permission.

Typeset by emc design ltd.

UNLOCK SECOND EDITION ADVISORY PANEL

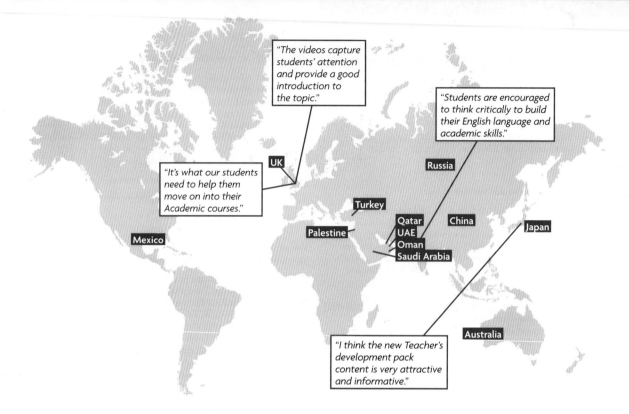

"The videos capture students' attention and provide a good introduction to the topic."

"Students are encouraged to think critically to build their English language and academic skills."

"It's what our students need to help them move on into their Academic courses."

"I think the new Teacher's development pack content is very attractive and informative."

UK
Russia
Turkey
Qatar
UAE
Oman
Saudi Arabia
Palestine
China
Japan
Mexico
Australia

We would like to thank the following ELT professionals all around the world for their support, expertise and input throughout the development of *Unlock* Second Edition:

Adnan Abu Ayyash, Birzeit University, Palestine	Takayuki Hara, Kagoshima University, Japan	Megan Putney, Dhofar University, Oman
Bradley Adrain, University of Queensland, Australia	Esengül Hasdemir, Atilim University, Turkey	Wayne Rimmer, United Kingdom
Sarah Ali, Nottingham Trent International College (NTIC), United Kingdom	Irina Idilova, Moscow Institute of Physics and Technology, Russia	Sana Salam, TED University, Turkey
Ana Maria Astiazaran, Colegio Regis La Salle, Mexico	Meena Inguva, Sultan Qaboos University, Oman	Setenay Şekercioglu, Işık University, Turkey
Asmaa Awad, University of Sharjah, United Arab Emirates	Vasilios Konstantinidis, Prince Sultan University, Kingdom of Saudi Arabia	Robert B. Staehlin, Morioka University, Japan
Jesse Balanyk, Zayed University, United Arab Emirates	Andrew Leichsenring, Tamagawa University, Japan	Yizhi Tang, Xueersi English, TAL Group, China
Lenise Butler, Universidad del Valle de México, Mexico	Alexsandra Minic, Modern College of Business and Science, Oman	Valeria Thomson, Muscat College, Oman
Esin Çağlayan, Izmir University of Economics, Turkey	Daniel Newbury, Fuji University, Japan	Amira Traish, University of Sharjah, United Arab Emirates
Matthew Carey, Qatar University, Qatar	Güliz Özgürel, Yaşar University, Turkey	Poh Leng Wendelkin, INTO London, United Kingdom
Eileen Dickens, Universidad de las Américas, Mexico	Özlem Perks, Istanbul Ticaret University, Turkey	Yoee Yang, The Affiliated High School of SCNU, China
Mireille Bassam Farah, United Arab Emirates	Claudia Piccoli, Harmon Hall, Mexico	Rola Youhia, University of Adelaide College, Australia
Adriana Ghoul, Arab American University, Palestine	Tom Pritchard, University of Edinburgh, United Kingdom	Long Zhao, Xueersi English, TAL Group, China
Burçin Gönülsen, Işık University, Turkey		